~ Won̶̶̶̶̶̶ ̶̶̶̶̶̶̶̶ ~

∽ Wonders on Ice ∽
Figure Skating in Minnesota

by

Moira F. Harris

POGO PRESS

Copyright © 2007 by Pogo Press

All rights reserved, including under all international and Pan American Copyright Conventions.

ISBN 10: 1-880654-35-0.
ISBN 13: 978-1-880654-35-4.
Library of Congress Control No. 2007930567.

Cover designed by Mighty Media.
Interior designed by Angela Wix.
Edited by Lindsey Cunneen.

Photographic credits:
Genny Burdette 8, 129 (below); Roy Blakey/IceStage Archive 37, 49, 56, 104, 107 (top), 108 (top), 109, 114, 115, 158, 159, 160; Janet Carpenter 64, 103, 144, 145, 147, 166; Tom Collins Enterprises 116, 117, 118; Del Conroy 63 (left), 66, 84, 111; Marion Curry 50 (below) 101, 102, 105, 107 (below), 108 (below), 110,112; Goodhue County Historical Society 33 (left); Moira F. Harris 6,7 (left), 18, 25, 36, 48, 63 (right), 74, 82 (left), 99, 130, 131, 142, 161; Paul Hempel 7(right); Janet Hoitomt 55 (both), 90 (both), 141; Virginia Johnson 75, 172; Anne Klein 21 (below), 51 (left), 126 (below), 127 (top), 138 (below); Marlys Larson 138, 153; Jerre LeTourneau 51 (right), 140 (both); Minnesota Historical Society 21, 46, 58, 65, 126 (top), 127 (below), 129 (top), 132 (below); MHS Strauss Skate Company Papers 30 (all), 31; MHS Ice Follies Collection 41, 100, 106; MHS Robert Uppgren Papers 146; *Minnesota Monthly* and Layne Kennedy, photographer 35; Minnesota State Fair History Museum 47, 49, 50 (top); Margaret Nordstog 59, 60, 61, 65, 72, 74, 82 (right), 128, 136; Molly Oberstar 77; Riedell Skates Inc. 33 (right), 34, 35; Rochester FSC 79 (bottom), 80, 81 (both), 169; St. Paul FSC 38, 62, 66 (right), 67, 68, 69, 162, 163 (top), 167, 168; Carole Shulman 79 (top), 170; Toni Swiggum 86, 87; Barbara Thomson 73, 74, 76 (both); TCFSA 53, 54, 85, 142, 143; Barb Yackel 163.

Cover image: Ruth Eastman, *The Skating Girl*, 1916. Courtesy of Eugene and Marilyn DiMartino.

Chapter-beginning illustrations for Chapters 2, 3, 4, 5, 6 are based on Rinky Dinks, a set of drawings created by Minnesota skater Vivi-Anne Hultén in 1977. Courtesy of Genny Burdette. Chapters 1 and 7 use a figure skater that appeared on the cover of the Children's Hospital Association Follies program of 1935. Courtesy of Dell Conroy.

Published by Pogo Press
An Imprint of Finney Company
8075 215th Street West
Lakeville, Minnesota 55044

www.finneyco.com
www.pogopress.com

Table of Contents

Introduction and Acknowledgments

M innesota, with its thousands of lakes and rivers, has long been home to winter sports. As soon as those lakes and rivers froze to a safe depth, men, women, and children ventured forth on the ice. Horses, cars, snowmobiles, sleds, hot air balloons, and sailboats could be raced on the frozen surface. Games like lacrosse, curling, polo, and hockey could be played on a plowed rink. Fishermen could tug their small colorful ice houses out from shore, cut a hole through the ice, and challenge the wary denizens of the deep. The uses for those icy expanses were many. One of the earliest sports and pastimes to be seen everywhere was, of course, ice skating.

Skating outdoors became a popular subject for artists, poets, and composers. Gilbert Stuart's *The Skater* is well-known, but probably equally familiar are Currier and Ives lithographs and Winslow Homer's wood engravings of skaters. Skating scenes appealed to trade card printers and artists designing greeting cards and sheet music covers. In the twentieth century, stamp designers have chosen skating scenes or skaters for issues

A Rafael Tuck oilette postcard based on a drawing by Lucien Davis, postmarked Christmas Day, 1911.

Trade cards and poster stamps often used skaters to advertise their products.

noting the Winter Olympics every four years and for annual Christmas stamps. Two Olympic gold medal winning figure skaters received one Minnesota accolade: their images appeared on boxes of General Mills' Wheaties breakfast cereal. It was Kristi Yamaguchi's turn in 1998, and four years later Sarah Hughes was the Wheaties champion.

Today each division of skating—figure, speed, and hockey—has developed many sub-specialties, both team and individual, so much so that a book about all forms of skating would be an enormous task, even one limited to Minnesota. This book, as its title indicates, deals only with figure skating, "fancy skating" as it was once called. The story begins virtually as soon as settlers started arriving in the area, some perhaps bringing skates with them. The tale continues with the story of the skating clubs, the exhibitions and skating shows, the products developed in Minnesota for use by skaters, the skating competitions held in the state and the titles earned by local skaters. The story features many well-known names and celebrated places. Skating history is a prominent part of our state's athletic heritage that deserves to be treasured by the skaters of today and remembered by the skating community of the future.

Model of a life-size bronze statue of Vivi-Anne Hultén by Janos Sovary. The original statue, completed in 1935, once stood in a park in Budapest, Hungary.

Figure skating is a sport, both recreational and competitive. It is often a lifetime activity, involving families and generations. It is entertainment, both amateur and professional. The Shipstad brothers and Oscar Johnson proved that in the 1930s with their very successful *Ice Follies*. Their show, based at first in Minnesota and using many Minnesota skaters in its casts, served as a prototype for the many traveling ice shows that followed. Professional shows and exhibitions, amateur follies, and carnivals are part of the Minnesota story as well.

After looking through numerous scrapbooks, programs, and piles of clippings, some opinions about the changes in press coverage of skating can be made. When newspapers had women's pages, stories about clubs were featured there. Reporters and columnists wrote for the entertainment pages about skaters and touring ice shows. Championship results could be read on the sports pages. Other reporters might note that the *Ice Follies* were in town and had sold out every performance once again. There might be a photo with a caption noting that a local skater had signed with the *Ice Capades* or the *Follies*. When local skaters came home for vacation after a season spent touring with the shows, this was news that attracted coverage. If the Sunday edition of the paper had a locally-produced magazine section, there might be a photo essay on Dorothy Lewis' show at the St. Regis Hotel in New York City or a panel of photos of a young girl learning to skate (and falling down) on a town lake. A fashion spread on the latest styles for skating that could be purchased at stores in town might fill a page. Skating generated news of interest to Minnesota readers for decades, but with today's newspapers filled with stories written elsewhere or reprinted from other sources, that is no longer the case. There are stories written about skaters and the sport, but far fewer than before despite the numbers of skaters, clubs, and events.

When a girl tumbles, her beau must rush to her side with expressions of pity, advised the St. Paul and Minneapolis Pioneer Press, *January 31, 1887, page 4.*

Many people have aided immeasurably on this project. They have shared information, photographs, memorabilia, and insights derived from years of involvement in the skating world. I am greatly indebted to Janet Carpenter, Lexie Kastner, Marion Curry, Marlys Larson, Anne Klein, Nancy Lund, Margaret Nordstog, Jean Pastor, Joan Brainard, Carole Shulman, Lynda Lubratt, Tom Collins, Nan Wright Conroy, Bette Snuggerud, Jane Schaber, Jerre LeTourneau, Gretchen Wilson, Jan Mattson, Bradley Kruse, Dan Riegelman, Alice Fitch, John Klindworth, Tamie Campbell, Janet Hoitomt, Del Conroy, Benjamin Wright, Barb Thomson, Ginny Johnson, Josephine Lawless, Vicky Fisher, and Genny Burdette. My special thanks go to Roy Blakey whose IceStage Archive is a treasure trove of photographs and skating ephemera supplemented by his knowledge of theatrical skating history.

Moira F. Harris
St. Paul, Minnesota
June 15, 2007

Preface

Some people figure skate for the pure pleasure, the feel of freedom and motion; some are "serious" skaters, taking lessons, passing structured tests, and entering competitions; still others simply observe and admire the beauty of the sport. All these facets are a part of Moira Harris' *Wonders on Ice: Figure Skating in Minnesota*. She has researched carefully the sport we Minnesotans love and of which we are so proud.

For one who has been involved in figure skating for nearly 70 years, I am overwhelmed by this book, with the rush of memories, as well as fascinated by the new facts and stories of people I never knew. Charlotte, the celebrated European skater, made a great impact on the Minnesota scene, as did an early appearance by Olympic champion Sonja Henie. Minnesota boys, the Shipstads and Johnson, creators of the famed *Ice Follies*, were idols of mine and I was always so proud of my friends who performed in their shows. The summer St. Paul Pop Concerts, presented three nights a week for many years, were a virtual training center for future Minnesota competitors and professional skaters. Skating to a live forty-five-piece orchestra in front of an audience of thousands was a unique and invaluable experience. How well I remember the afternoon skating practice sessions while the orchestra was rehearsing its semi-classical music for that evening's Pop Concert. We skaters never jumped higher nor spun faster. It was inspiring and magical!

Moira writes about the old Minneapolis Arena. What a cold rink… we would warm our skating boots and gloves on the radiators before and between sessions, and drink hot cocoa from thermoses. But what a magnificent sheet of ice, hand swept by a rink crew and then flooded with warm water (no Zamboni in those days). One of my most cherished memories is going into that dark rink before school and "cutting" school figures into untouched ice. It was so quiet you could hear your blade changing edges and sometimes the ice would make a cracking sound beneath you. I loved those moments.

To have grown up in the traditions of Minnesota figure skating was a privilege. We had world class coaches and there were always talented skaters to admire and emulate, some of whom became our mentors. There is a camaraderie amongst Minnesota skaters and also amongst the judges and officials, and life-long friendships are formed. These traditions remain and Minnesota figure skating is currently strong and thriving, from toddlers to adults, synchronized teams to international competitors. And let us not forget the many recreational skaters who just "love to skate."

Wonders on Ice tells the stories of past and present Minnesota figure skating. We now have a history, in words and pictures, of a great skating community. Many thanks to Moira Harris for her fine work.

Janet Gerhauser Carpenter
Minnetonka, Minnesota
June 25, 2007

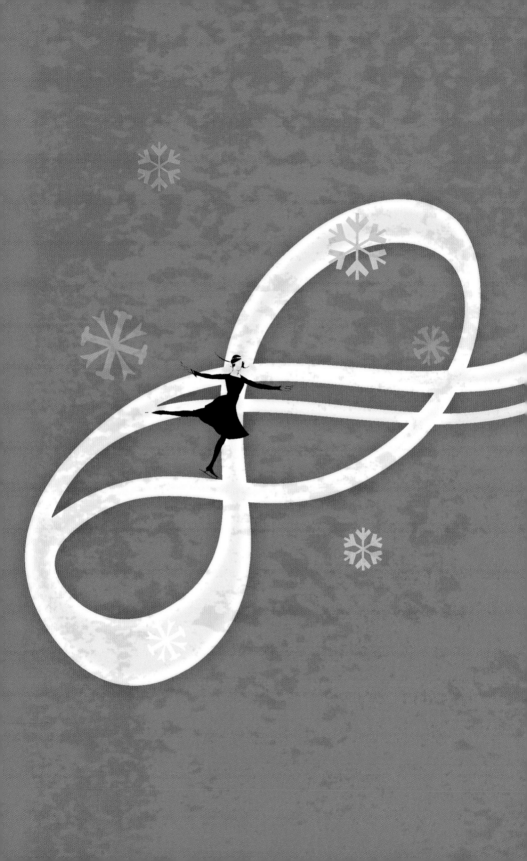

Chapter One

In the Beginning: Sites and Influences

Ice skating was one of the most popular sports of the nineteenth century. For Minnesotans it was an accessible pastime, which could be practiced on rivers and nearby lakes from late fall until spring approached. Once the ice was thick enough, rinks or simply paths were kept open for skaters. As one St. Paul writer described his childhood, all he had to do was "sling a pair of skates on his back and start out for the river." There he would meet other boys, and "shoot off on his shining blades for thirty or forty miles, and return in time for supper." Roller skating, with its wooden rollers rumbling on wooden floors, was not like the sharp ring of a skate blade on the ice. Nor were the electric lights, the crowd, the hurly-burly and the stifling air of the indoor rink like the silvery moon and solemn silence of the frozen lake.[1]

Frank O'Brien remembered the winter of 1860-61 as long but filled with the fun of skating on the river.[2] For this Minneapolis boy, the favorite place for skating was on the Mississippi River from the suspension bridge, up the river, and around Nicollet Island to the channel on the east side. If snow covered the ice, boys from St. Anthony (across the river from Minneapolis) would shovel it off.

Skaters wore "turnovers or stub-toes." These skates had "grooved runners with heel corks, and straps that were secured so tightly upon the feet that circulation of the blood in those parts was next to impossible…" Turnovers had brass knobs and were more expensive than the stub-toe skates. Boys wearing stub-toes fastened them on their feet with tarred rope stretched tight with inserts of cordwood to make the ropes fast. Girls and boys would wear hand-knit skating socks over their boots or shoes to keep warm.

In the evening huge bonfires illuminated the scene and surrounded the skaters in clouds of smoke. The wood for the bonfires, O'Brien wrote, might have come from Colonel Stevens' woodpile. Or from Mr. Gray the druggist's barrels, or even from Captain Tapper the Ferryman's fence, but he didn't really want to say. Sometimes a brass band would even find its way to the riverside to serenade the skaters with waltzes.

Out on the ice, quite a few skaters expertly cut "pigeon wings, monograms, backward circles or scrolls," figures that by this Civil War era were already widely known to American figure skaters. By the time O'Brien was writing about that winter, forty years had passed. Now, he noted, the city provided rinks in Loring and Powderhorn parks where the ice was kept free of snow, electric lights shone on the rink, and skaters could change from shoes to skates inside warming houses. It was all very nice and modern, but skating on the river had been invigorating and glorious fun.

By 1910, when Melvin Frank was a boy, skating on the river was no longer safe as the water did not completely freeze. The sawmill owners kept pools open so they could move their logs around in the "hot pot" system.[3] So rather than using the Mississippi as a rink, skaters headed to the parks where baseball diamonds were flooded by the city park board in winter. Frank and his friends skated at Farview Park at 29th and Lyndale Avenues North in Minneapolis. Skating was often a problem for Frank because of his troublesome skates:

> My first skates were steel clamp-ons that attached to
> everyday shoes. Web straps helped hold the skates on
> and at the same time lent support to the skater's ankles.
> Those skates were the bane of my life. I would get them
> on with painstaking effort and take to the ice with
> other kids. Just when the hockey game or tag was
> going great, I would find myself on one skate, with the
> other dragging from the strap. And so I would limp
> back, rather humiliated, to the warming house and
> repeat the struggle to get the skate attached securely.
> The clamp had to be adjusted to the size of the shoe
> sole and heel, fitted on, and the strap set and tightened.
> Not long after I returned to the ice, sure enough the
> skate came loose.[4]

Screw clamp skates were not much of an improvement and, although shoe skates were available, his father could not afford to buy them. So shoe skates had to wait until Frank had earned enough money to buy his own pair of Nestor Johnsons.

Various events would spur the growth of interest in Minnesota skating. There were the visits of Axel Paulsen, the Norwegian speed skater

The Winter Carnival clubs enjoyed skating on the frozen Mississippi River near the Wabasha bridge. Northwest Illustrated Magazine, *Winter Carnival edition, 1887.*

in 1890, and Charlotte, the German skating star in 1917, and there was the birth of the St. Paul Winter Carnival in 1886. St. Paul's famous festival began when Montreal, which had already sponsored a successful winter event, cancelled its upcoming festival due to an outbreak of illness. For St. Paul business leaders and newspapermen, this was a chance to boost the fortunes of their city by inviting the world to see their town in winter. Publicity and increased tourism were the goals, but at the same time the city's residents discovered the fun of the outdoors, even when the temperature headed to many degrees below zero, as it did in 1885-86.

A carnival needs pageantry, parties, and parades. Montreal's carnival had an ice palace as its focal point and locus of activities. Plans for the ice palace that the Canadians were unable to build were supplied to St. Paul. From Canada came many ideas for carnival programming and events. Montreal had encouraged its citizens to form sports clubs that could then participate in the carnival, especially through marching in its parades. St. Paulites quickly formed clubs devoted to tobogganing, skiing, snowshoeing, and skating.

— As Merrily We Glide —

Over half of the Carnival club's members were women who "insisted on having all the fun there is in the Carnival."

The *St. Paul and Minneapolis Pioneer Press* reported:

The Carnival Skating club now numbers 112 gentlemen and 75 ladies—the limit of its membership. The only infelicitous thing about this is that there are five other skating clubs and but two small rinks on the palace grounds for the whole six, with over 350 members. The clubs very much desire that the association [the organizers of the Carnival] should furnish them with a rink on the river. This could be done without a great deal of expense, and would doubtless add much to the popularity of the carnival. The clubs do not feel as though they desire to go to their expense themselves for there would be no way of making the rink private, and the clubs would be thus paying for facilities for furnishing amusement for the general public which, they claim, would be a manifest injustice.[5]

In addition to the Carnival skating club, there were skating groups named Palace, Tosaka, Standard, Alaska, and Rainbow, a club for ladies only.

There were other expenses for the skating club members. They needed uniforms, torches to carry in the evening parades, and skates. The uniform for a man included a coat and pants, a toque or tasseled hat, sash, stockings, and moccasins. Ladies wore a dress, a toque, sash, stockings, and either boots or moccasins. Hats, coats, and muffs could be trimmed with fur. The colors selected for the Carnival club men's uniforms were blue for the coat and pants, red for the trimming, and a red sash and leggings. The ladies wore red and white with a blue sash and cap. Both sexes had badges with the CSC monogram of the club on their jackets. The material used for uniforms was thick blanket wool. One blanket could usually be cut into at least two uniforms. Local Sioux Indians often fashioned the moccasins. Skates ranged in price from 75¢ for a boy's model to $7-$10 for a better grade nickel blade. Local dealers had plenty of skates on hand, reported the newspaper, and uniforms could be made by tailors in a day.[6]

These skating clubs took part in all four of the nineteenth century Winter Carnivals (1886, 1887, 1888, and 1896), marching in the parades each year and enjoying the rinks inside the palace grounds. Various races for speed skaters were scheduled in the 1886 Carnival as well as an exhibition for the fancy skaters. In the latter event a man who triumphed won a gold medal; the best female skater won a toilet set; the best couple skating was rewarded with pairs of skates. Accounts do not indicate the rules for judging or who gave the verdicts.

Despite the enthusiastic response to St. Paul's early Carnivals, no further festivals were held until 1916. The clubs disbanded with the exception of the Nushka club.[7] Its members were

A fancy skater could do a pigeon wing, figure eight, spread eagle, grape vine, and end his exhibition by writing his name with his blade.

enthusiastic about all winter sports as well as wintertime social gatherings. Lack of money and erratic weather conditions (it was warm in January!) halted the events until Louis Hill, president of the Great Northern Railway, created the city's Outdoor Sports Carnivals in 1916 and 1917.

Recognized stars from the winter sports world have often appeared in Minnesota for competition and shows. Their visits have certainly brought attention to the sport of figure skating. Axel Paulsen (1855-1938), the great Norwegian skater, was one of the earliest to come. He was in America to compete against other speed skaters for the world championship. A group of Norwegian Americans invited him to Minneapolis in January 1890 for a best two-out-of-three series of races against the Canadian Hugh McCormick. The first race, fifteen miles in

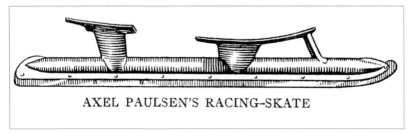

AXEL PAULSEN'S RACING–SKATE

From Irving Brokaw's The Art of Skating *(1926), page 26.*

length, was held on what was called the Palace rink, and betting on the outcome was heavy. Paulsen won, as many had expected. The race was marred in the homestretch when a chair was thrown on the ice and McCormick stumbled trying to avoid it.[8] According to one account, Paulsen made the Twin Cities his American headquarters. He was often seen skating on local rinks such as the Pillbox at 11th and Robert streets, and on Lake Como where he was said to have done trick jumps over a team of mules.[9] It was Paulsen's invention of the axel, a jump that is performed forwards rather than backwards, that assures his presence in figure skating history.

Just before America's entry into World War I, Louis Hill felt it was time to boost St. Paul's reputation as a winter sports capital. Although the festivals he headed followed in the tradition of those organized earlier, he insisted that they be called Outdoor Sports Carnivals rather than Winter Carnivals as otherwise potential visitors might be deterred from coming if they imagined they would have to contend with snow and bitterly cold weather. His festivals, said Mr. Hill, would be "hot times" for the city. Back again would be parades, sports competitions, and ice palaces (built more like Western stockades than the immense edifices of the Canadian variety). Businesses were asked to organize marching groups, nominate a pretty employee as a candidate for Queen of the Snows, and sponsor motorized, not horse-drawn, floats. Many businesses featured the carnival logo in their advertising and one, the Theo Hamm Brewery, used a skater, arguing that beer was a healthy drink for sports enthusiasts.

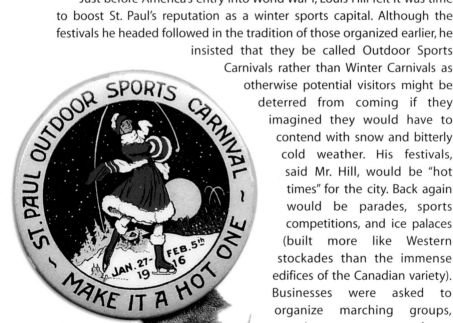

Louis Moen's Carnival Girl appeared on everything from buttons to billboards promoting the St. Paul Outdoor Sports Carnival of 1916.

Charlotte demonstrates the Charlotte stop. From Irving Brokaw's,
The Art of Skating *(1926), page 126.*

One St. Paul newspaper reported that costumes for skating had changed. "This season is the first that America has accepted this sport as a social accomplishment."[10] Not only were there local firms making skate boots and blades, but many stores offered clothing suitable for the recreational skater. For sale were belted coats, plain tailored skirts, corduroy suits in Norfolk style, skating coats in short or three-quarter length. Plaids or stripes were appropriate for skirts and the well-dressed skater wore a middy blouse in wool flannel with trimmings or in silk crepe de chine.

The image of the 1916 Carnival was the Carnival Girl, a figure skater dressed in a red coat trimmed with white fur. She was featured on the thousands of posters, postcards, poster stamps, and buttons produced to promote the festival. A Minneapolis model, Irene Grayston, was selected to embody the Carnival Girl.[11] She, rather than any of the 100-plus queen candidates, led the Grand March with the Carnival king (Boreas Rex) at the festival ball.

The next year an actual figure skating star was in St. Paul just prior to the opening of the Carnival. Charlotte Oelschlagel (1898-1984) had begun skating in Germany at age seven. She skated in indoor ice ballets in Berlin at age twelve. Charles Dillingham, an American entrepreneur, invited her to New York City where she and her show *Hip, Hip, Hooray!* had a triumphant

425-performance run at the New York Hippodrome.[12] The show closed and went on the road to seven cities. *Hip, Hip, Hooray!* opened in St. Paul on January 15, 1917, and it featured Charlotte (whose last name was seldom given), John Philip Sousa (the March King) and his band, forty other skaters, Chin Chin the baby elephant, and Toto the chimpanzee. It was the first touring skating entertainment ever seen in St. Paul.

Hippodrome shows, wrote Charles M. Flandrau, the art critic of the *St. Paul Pioneer Press*, were hard to classify as they incorporated so many elements. "Part spectacle, part ballet, part glorified vaudeville, part circus, part band concert—at times separately, and then again all together—they are given to providing an evening of brilliant color, elaborate stage effects, extravagant scenic ingenuity, bewildering rhythm, and flashes of individual talent that at the end of every climax leaves one speculating as to what can possibly come next."[13] Newspapers were fascinated with the show. One report mentioned the effort involved as the Auditorium staff changed the wood floor used for a forest dance scene to the ice needed for Charlotte's ice ballet.[14] A skating pond, 96 by 45 feet, was placed on the stage floor. An eighteen-inch-deep tank lined with cork sat on the floor. Then came a system of $1\frac{1}{2}$ inch pipes holding brine and ammonia which helped freeze the water to ice. Another layer of cork protected the ice while the forest scenery was set on top of it.

Other reports focused on Charlotte.

To celebrate her presence, a welcoming Carnival parade took place on Monday morning. Charlotte, Sousa, the Carnival king (Boreas Rex), the mayor of St. Paul, and Minnesota's governor, J.A.A. Burnquist, greeted the marchers of the non-motorized parade as they passed by the steps of the state capitol. That evening the show opened, and the following morning Charlotte was supposed to greet a number of St. Paul society women at tea. But she didn't. Instead of meeting them in the Auditorium, Charlotte remained in her hotel room with her right foot immersed in a tub of almost boiling water from Lake Vadnais. She had fallen and hurt her ankle while pirouetting in the "Flirting at St. Moritz" number the night before.[15] While the society ladies had to be content with feeding peanuts to Chin Chin the elephant and seeing the backstage preparations for the show, at least a few of them remained interested in skating. They were among those who would begin the Children's Hospital Association and help organize the Children's Hospital *Ice Follies* a decade and a half later.

Charlotte is remembered for her artistic skating, her athleticism, and because she wore skates like those of Jackson Haines, the American skater who introduced dancing on skates to Europe. She was the first woman to perform Axel Paulsen's jump and she invented the Charlotte stop, a spiral

Governor J.A.A.Burnquist, Boreas Rex II J.P.Ridler, John Philip Sousa, and Charlotte watched the Carnival parade from the state capitol steps on January 15, 1917.

which ends with the skater's head down (Charlotte's long hair touched the ice) and her free leg extended high in the air. Her "Dying Swan" number, said to have been derived from the solo danced by Anna Pavlova, the ballerina, was another famous routine.[16]

Before enclosed arenas or rinks were built, skaters continued to use the lakes for recreation and the occasional skating party. In *Main Street*, first published in 1920, Sinclair Lewis describes his heroine Carol Kennicott's effort to introduce a skating party as an activity to her new neighbors in Gopher Prairie, a fictional town located north of the Twin Cities. They accept her invitation to skate on Plover Lake and one man even traces figure eights on the ice. But when other winter sports are suggested for

Skating as Carol Kennicott hoped to see it in Gopher Prairie. Here the scene is Cedar Lake in Minneapolis, 1923.

the social calendar, Mrs. Kennicott's plans are rejected. People in St. Paul might enjoy ice skating, but in Gopher Prairie they preferred an indoor evening of bridge-whist.[17]

While other Minnesota artists may have drawn skating scenes, it was a St. Paul-born cartoonist whose characters most often found their way to an ice rink just as he did. Although hockey was more often the sport for the *Peanuts* characters of Charles Schulz (1922-2000), the cartoonist did create story lines involving figure skating. In January 1978 a month-long series featured Peppermint Patty as an aspiring figure skater. She practiced her loops and figures outside, under the watchful eye of her crabby coach Snoopy and her admiring friend Marcy. When hockey players tried to usurp her space, she told them off just as other skaters might want to do.

Schulz had a lifelong interest in skating and hockey. He illustrated the program cover for the 1981 U.S. Nationals held in San Diego. In that instance it is Snoopy who skates. Across the street from The Charles M. Schulz Museum in Santa Rosa, California, is a hockey rink that Schulz built and where he often spent time. In 2007 the museum exhibited a number of strips related to skating in an exhibit titled *Peanuts on Ice*. After the cartoonist died in 2000, the city of St. Paul named its hockey rink in Highland Park in his memory. In its lobby is a fiberglass statue named *Slapshot* showing Snoopy in hockey gear. Schulz was elected posthumously to the USFSA Hall of Fame in 2006.

In another fictional small Minnesota town, volunteer firemen flooded the ice to make a smooth rink by the beach. Colored lights hung in a "V" from the warming house to the pole on the diving dock. Lake Wobegon skaters put on their skates next to a wood stove in what had once been a chicken house that still had "a faint recollection of chickens" emanating from the floor. Then the skaters "teetered down the ramp" and glided off to recorded organ music played through a Zenith console put out on the ice, as Garrison Keillor wrote.[18]

In Chisago City skaters used the lake for a rink when the ice was safely thick. At least one inch, Herb Johnson remembered, although that "was probably not enough, but we used it and did our skating." Cattails and other brush were collected to begin a bonfire. The town had another rink made by flooding land near the Northern Pacific railroad tracks. A shack with a wood stove served as a warming house and benches were set alongside the rink for the skaters to use. Flood lights made night skating possible.[19] This rink was used as the setting for the coronation of Chisago City's winter carnival queen in 1948. A requirement for queen contestants was the ability to skate.

Poets have also been inspired by skating as this verse, published at the time of the first St. Paul Winter Carnival indicates:

> The skaters are out on the ice shod with steel;
> As graceful as sea-gulls they circle and wheel.
> Behold that young maiden so charming and sweet,
> And see the light flash from her swift-gliding feet;
> The sunlight reflected, this fine winter day:
> God bless the fair skater! Forever, I say![20]

Skating outdoors on Lake Wobegon was quite similar to practicing the sport in the Twin Cities. Skaters in Minneapolis headed to Cedar, Loring, or Powderhorn lakes, or Lake of the Isles. In St. Paul skaters found cleared ice on Como or Phalen lakes and an early rink known as the Hollow at Kent and Mackubin streets. Enthusiasm for skating had grown, another writer noted. "Almost any morning a gay set of young women may be seen in their picturesque costumes on the University club rink and each evening finds the different sets of friends on skates at the Hippodrome, at Lake Como, and at Dellwood."[21] Outdoor skating could safely be done from whenever the lakes froze in the fall until they melted in the spring. When indoor facilities were first built, their seasons lasted from late fall to early spring.

As Everett McGowan commented to an interviewer, "Where I lived we had very long winters, and everybody put on ice skates for the cold months. The firemen would flood a space for a rink, or you would take your shovel, and clear a pond, but winter meant skating."[22] McGowan began as a speed skater, then played hockey, and finally donned figure skates. His career included medals won in races and years as an adagio ice dancer (his partner was his wife Ruth) with *Holiday on Ice*, *Ice Capades*, and his own troupe, the *McGowan and Mack Ice Review*.

In 1924 the city of Rochester planned to open a municipal outdoor ice skating rink early in January. First too much snow fell, and then the weather turned warm. But finally conditions were right and the formal opening of the rink took place. The rink measured one and a half blocks long by a half block wide. Lights were strung around the rink to allow night skating, and a warming house, with a separate room for lady skaters, provided for comfort. To maintain the surface of the rink, the account continued:

> A quantity of hot water is kept on hand all of the time
> and as quickly as a bit of shell ice is chipped off by the
> skaters, it is immediately repaired by pouring hot water
> into the hole left. When the rink is planed to remove the

rough spots hot water is sprinkled over it by sprinklers
on hand sleds. The hot water thaws the ice around the
rough places and they freeze over smoothly.[23]

The first indoor facility was not built originally for skaters, but for livestock and horses. The Hippodrome at the Minnesota State Fairgrounds in St. Paul was designed in Spanish mission style with a red tile roof by W. M. Kenyon, a Minneapolis architect.[24] It opened in 1906. A few years later Gale Brooke and Ed Dickinson had the idea that the Hippodrome's large arena, measuring 277 by 121 feet, could be flooded for skating. After the floor had been cleared of the bark and soil trod on by the animals, the doors and windows were left open and the arena was flooded. In addition to its large floor space, the Hippodrome could seat 7,500 people for hockey, skating, and shows. The Hippodrome thus became the birthplace of indoor skating and, because of the early carnivals and follies held there, it witnessed the beginning of theatrical skating in Minnesota. Until 1924, when the Arena opened in Minneapolis, it was the only place to skate inside in winter.

In a memoir included in the Minnesota Historical Society's online histories of the 1930s and 1940s, Dorothy Snell Curtis wrote about figure skating in the Hippodrome.[25] Mrs. Curtis is the granddaughter of John Strauss, the blade maker. She began her skating life with heavy wide blades mounted on black boots. She skated on Lake Owasso, whose ice, she wrote, was "at its most beautiful, a dark sapphire," or on a frozen playground in St. Paul. Serious skaters needed indoor ice for practice and that she found at the Hippodrome. On Saturdays she took lessons from Roy Shipstad and then, with other neophyte skaters, there were games:

> We played our first game of the day on that shining,
> slick sheet as, dropping to our backsides after a good
> sprint, we tried for the longest, fastest slide. After our
> lessons and as more skaters arrived, we formed a samba
> line behind the lead skater, who had to be strong, or we
> staged foot races or played tag, or at top speed
> squatted on one skate to 'shoot the duck' or, best of all,
> played crack-the-whip.[26]

The Hippodrome ice was frozen when the outdoor temperature grew cold enough to do the job by simply opening the doors and windows. Dorothy Curtis remembered the cold as "outrageous. Heavily wrapped against it one was too constricted to move well; lightly wrapped and one was too cold."[27] Skaters could warm up when free skating, but the slow pace of doing figures made it difficult to practice those maneuvers for long periods. Yet, she felt, skating at such cold temperatures probably helped develop strong, long strides and deep hard edges.[28]

The Arena, at 29th Street and Dupont Avenue South in Minneapolis, was an ice rink from November to May and offered roller skating in the summer. Lyle Wright, a Canadian who came to Minneapolis in 1919, owned the Arena with his partners George Drake and George Heller. Wright, a former hockey player, served as the manager of the Arena.

The Minneapolis professional ice hockey team, the Millers, played their games at the Arena, the Figure Skating Club of Minneapolis made it their home rink, and the *Ice Follies* did their shows at the Arena for many years. Often the *Follies'* touring schedule ended in Minneapolis in May. Then the company took a month-long vacation and the many Minnesota cast members went home. Sonja Henie made her first Minnesota appearance as an amateur at the Arena in 1930 and returned for another show with many future *Ice Follies* stars in 1934.

The St. Paul Auditorium Arena was the third and newest of the major ice skating venues. The Auditorium was built on Fifth Street west of Rice Park and acclaimed as the largest municipal auditorium in the country at the time. Within a few decades it was considered too small. An arena was added in 1931 that could seat 15,000 people, double the capacity of the Hippodrome. Its ice sheet area—224 by 100 feet—was smaller. With

Postcard view of the St. Paul Auditorium's ornate interior. The Auditorium opened in 1907 and was demolished in 1982.

pride it was said that it only took ten hours to flood the arena for skating or hockey and less than two hours to remove the ice.[29] The arena, often referred to as the Annex, and now named for the civil rights leader Roy Wilkins, served as home ice for many years for the St. Paul Figure Skating Club and welcomed the St. Paul Pop Concerts from 1939-74.

The Auditorium once stood where the Ordway Musical Theater stands now and a Rainbow grocery store occupies the old location of the Minneapolis Arena. In 1986, to mark the 50th anniversary of the *Ice Follies*, a plaque donated by former *Follies* skaters was placed on the wall near the grocery store's main entrance. Twenty years had also gone by since the Arena met the wrecking ball in May 1966.

Once figure skaters had the Hippodrome, the Arena, and the Auditorium for skating, they seldom returned to outdoor lakes to skate and practice figures. The clubs made ice time available indoors, dividing the rinks into "patches" where school figures could be practiced. Ice hockey, speed skating, and some of the long blade skaters continued to skate outdoors by choice. As the odd winter of 2007 proved, however, a frozen lake in January is not a given in Minnesota. The National Pond Hockey championships were scheduled for one Minneapolis lake and had to be moved to another lake when the ice proved too thin and open water was visible.

For some skaters the experience of skating on a frozen lake in northern Minnesota can still be a magical moment. Nature writer Sigurd Olson described coming upon a newly frozen lake one day in December. It had frozen with no snow cover and without wind to create ridges or uneven patches in its surface. It was clear and smooth. He skated its length in delight. It was late afternoon and as he skated, he realized that he was passing through shafts of color created by the Northern lights. "I knew," he wrote, "the joy that skating and skiing can give, freedom of movement beyond myself."[30]

✳ ❄ ✳ ❄ ✳ ❄ ✳ ❄

1. E.V. Smalley. *St. Paul and Minneapolis Pioneer Press: Winter Carnival Edition* (January 31, 1887), 3-4. Line drawings on pages 9, 16, 17 of this volume appeared with this article.
2. Frank G. O'Brien. *Minnesota Pioneer Sketches: From the Personal Recollections and Observations of a Pioneer Resident.* Minneapolis: H. H. S. Rowell (1904), 236-8.
3. Melvin Frank. "Sawmill City Boyhood," *Minnesota History* (Winter 1980), 148.
4. Frank, *ibid.*
5. "Skating: An invigorating sport," *St. Paul and Minneapolis Pioneer Press,* January 31, 1886, 3-4.
6. "Carnival Notes," *St. Paul and Minneapolis Pioneer Press,* January 30, 1886, 8.
7. Virginia L. Rahm. "The Nushka Club," *Minnesota History* 43 (Winter 1973), 303-307.
8. *Minneapolis Tribune,* January 1, 1890.
9. *Pioneer Magazine,* November 6, 1938, 5.
10. "Skating Brings in New Fashions," *St. Paul Dispatch,* January 3, 1916, 7.

11. Moira F. Harris. *Fire & Ice: The History of the St. Paul Winter Carnival*. St. Paul: Pogo Press (2003), 40.

12. James R. Hines. *Figure Skating: A History*. Urbana: University of Illinois Press (2006), 136. The idea to invite Charlotte came from Irving Brokaw. See his book, *The Art of Skating* (1926), 10.

13. C. M. Flandrau, *St. Paul Pioneer Press*, January 14, 1917, section 3, page 7.

14. *St. Paul Pioneer Press*, January 14, 1917, section 4, page 6.

15. "Queen of Skaters Soaks Her Foot As Society Waits," *St. Paul Dispatch*, January 16, 1917, 1.

16. Hines, *op cit*, 138.

17. Sinclair Lewis, *Main Street*. Limited Edition. Chicago: Lakeside Press (1937), 67.

18. Garrison Keillor, *Lake Wobegon Days*. New York: Viking (1985), 21-2.

19. J. Herbert Johnson. "Growing Up in Chisago City: One Man's Recollection of Boyhood Memories," Manuscript (2005).

20. J. W. Boxell. "Winter Carnival Rhymes," *Northwest Magazine, Winter Carnival edition*, 1887, 3.

21. *St. Paul Pioneer Press*, January 5, 1917, 7.

22. *Sullivan County Democrat* (Calicoon, New York), December 20, 1979, 1A.

23. *Rochester Post-Bulletin,* January 12, 1924, 5.

24. Diane Kempner. "When Skating was Hipp," *Minnesota Monthly* (December 1986), 67.

25. Dorothy Snell Curtis. "Changing Edges," *In Their Words: Stories of Minnesota's Greatest Generation*, Minnesota Historical Society. Currently available online at www.mngreatestgeneration.org.

26. Curtis, *ibid*, 2.

27. Curtis, *ibid*.

28. Curtis, *ibid*.

29. *St. Paul Pioneer Press*, March 22, 1936, section 1, page 9.

30. Sigurd F. Olson. *The Singing Wilderness*. New York: Alfred A. Knopf (1976), 184.

Chapter Two

What a Skater Needs

Nineteenth century skaters needed winter clothing and skates. The clothes a skater wore depended on fashion, expense, and the weather, but could usually be found locally. Skates were another matter. The metal blades with their wooden tops were shipped from East Coast cities. As interest in skating grew, local business leaders realized that they could supply the market instead. For many years the most important maker of skate blades was John E. Strauss (1856-1946) of St. Paul.

Strauss was born in Osterode, Germany, and served an apprenticeship to a locksmith. When his training was completed, he headed south to Switzerland and then to Italy. He left Naples in 1878 for America. Once he had arrived in St. Paul, he opened a business at 16 West Third Street (now known as Kellogg Boulevard). There he repaired and made bicycles in the summer and worked on locks and safes in the winter. As the craze for bicycles waned, he turned to making skates. The first Strauss pair of skates was sold to the skater Harley Davidson in 1890.

That year Axel Paulsen made his visit to Minneapolis and raced against Hugh McCormick on maple-topped skates. A. O. Smith, another St. Paul firm, made tubular skates at the time and Strauss thought they could stand improvement. Using a special type of steel, which he had learned to temper in a process that made it hard as glass, Strauss entered into the skate-making world. His first skates were for speed skaters like Paulsen.

In 1914 he invented a type of closed toe figure skate with a one-piece blade and three stanchions to attach it to the sole plate. Dorothy Curtis wrote of her grandfather's innovative design that gave the blade stability. Placing the teeth of the blade underneath the boot rather than in front of it made possible the eventual development of multiple turn jumps. "Skaters found they were able to jump high enough to turn twice or three times before landing safely on a three-stanchion blade that did not twang like a plucked string on impact."[1]

Above: John Strauss stands in the
doorway of his St. Paul store on
Third Street, circa 1887.

Right: Sonja Henie thanked
Mr. Strauss for his skates with
her photograph,
autographed and dated
February 28, 1935.

To Mr. J. E. Strauss
With kindliest regards
from
Sonja Henie
28-2-35

In a letter to the firm from Oslo, Sonja Henie wrote ordering more skates like those she had purchased earlier, but with some modifications. She enclosed photographs and added a note to Mr. Strauss that read, "I von the European championship in St. Moritz and the Worlds in Wienna on the skates made by you. I have been very satisfied with them."[2]

Many figure skating champions wore Strauss skates. Ernie Pyle, the nationally syndicated columnist, visited the Strauss store and wrote:

> They say that nearly every skater of any prominence in
> America from Sonja Henie on down, uses Strauss skates.
> And they all come from a little, old-fashioned, cluttered-
> up, antiquish workroom in St. Paul that resembles a
> country blacksmith shop.[3]

The Strauss firm remained in St. Paul until 1969. It then moved to a new building in Maplewood, at 1751 East Cope, where some of the early skate blades and skates made by the firm are displayed on a wall above the repair window. Production at that time was about 450 pairs per year. The company was sold to a nephew of the founder in 1981. During the lifetimes of both Strauss father and son, virtually every columnist for the local papers wrote about their firm. In one newspaper report photographs

John Strauss shows skate blades to Evelyn Chandler, the Ice Follies star, circa 1934.

Oberhamer advertisement from skating show program, 1965.

of Mr. Strauss Sr. making skate blades appeared as a panel on the front page just below the headline.[4]

To go with the Strauss blades, a skater often chose boots from the F. Oberhamer Shoe Company, another St. Paul firm. Joan Brainard remembers being told to wear the boots barefoot for a week before having the blades attached. This softened the leather. Other skaters spoke with pride about owning the boots or with regret that they had never been able to afford them. The Oberhamer firm was no longer in business by the late 1980s. A bank sold the company to an investor who was convicted of embezzlement and jailed in 1988.

A second type of blades was made by the Olympiad firm, at 859 North Deppe Street, in St. Paul. "They actually cost less to own," read the advertisements. They were endorsed by Robin Lee, five times men's national skating champion from St. Paul. The Olympiad blades, made by the Blochinger family, were excellent and used by skaters nationwide.

In Red Wing, Minnesota, a major business for over a century has been the making of boots and shoes. When the Red Wing Shoe Company celebrated its centennial in 2004, marking the event was a display of decorated fiberglass boots marching along the city's sidewalks for the summer. One employee of the Red Wing company was a machinist and foreman in addition to being a skater. Paul Riedell (1906-1987) designed his own boots in 1936 and then made pairs for his friends. He and his wife Sophie often demonstrated figure skating at local rinks, so they knew what a skater needed. With company permission he put his name on boots he

Left: Paul Riedell prepares cardboard cutouts for boots from a style sheet, circa 1960.

Right: The Riedell firm has made boots for figure skaters, bowlers, curlers, and roller skaters. Here all the styles are worn by Paul Riedell.

made. Interest from customers led Paul Riedell to begin his own company in 1945, opening a factory on Dakota Street, near Main, to manufacture skating boots in Red Wing.

The business grew, so Riedell Shoes Inc. moved to a larger space and finally to its current location in the Red Wing Industrial Park along Highway 61, north of the city.[5] The management team now represents the third generation of the family, the grandsons of Paul Riedell. The product line has included shoes for bowling and curling, but the main focus continues to be the sometimes gaudy boots for roller skating and the sober beige or white boots for the figure skater. Originally Riedell made only the boots, but the firm has acquired manufacturers of blades and wheels so the assembly can be done in Red Wing. Demand, said Riedell vice president Dan Riegelman, is often cyclical. Just as some say attention was brought to figure skating by the Tonya Harding–Nancy Kerrigan episode, roller skating has garnered interest from the doings of the Derby Girls.

Just as a Sonja Henie or a Robin Lee once signed photographs showing skates they wore, a lobby cabinet at Riedell's displays photographs of Michelle Kwan, Rhianna Brammeier, Johnny Weir, and Eliot Halverson wearing Riedell skates. Courtney Sayther wrote her thanks to Riedell on a March 1998 cover of *Minnesota Monthly* that pictured her in a layback spin.

Eliot Halverson, 2007 U.S. national junior champion, appears in a Riedell ad.

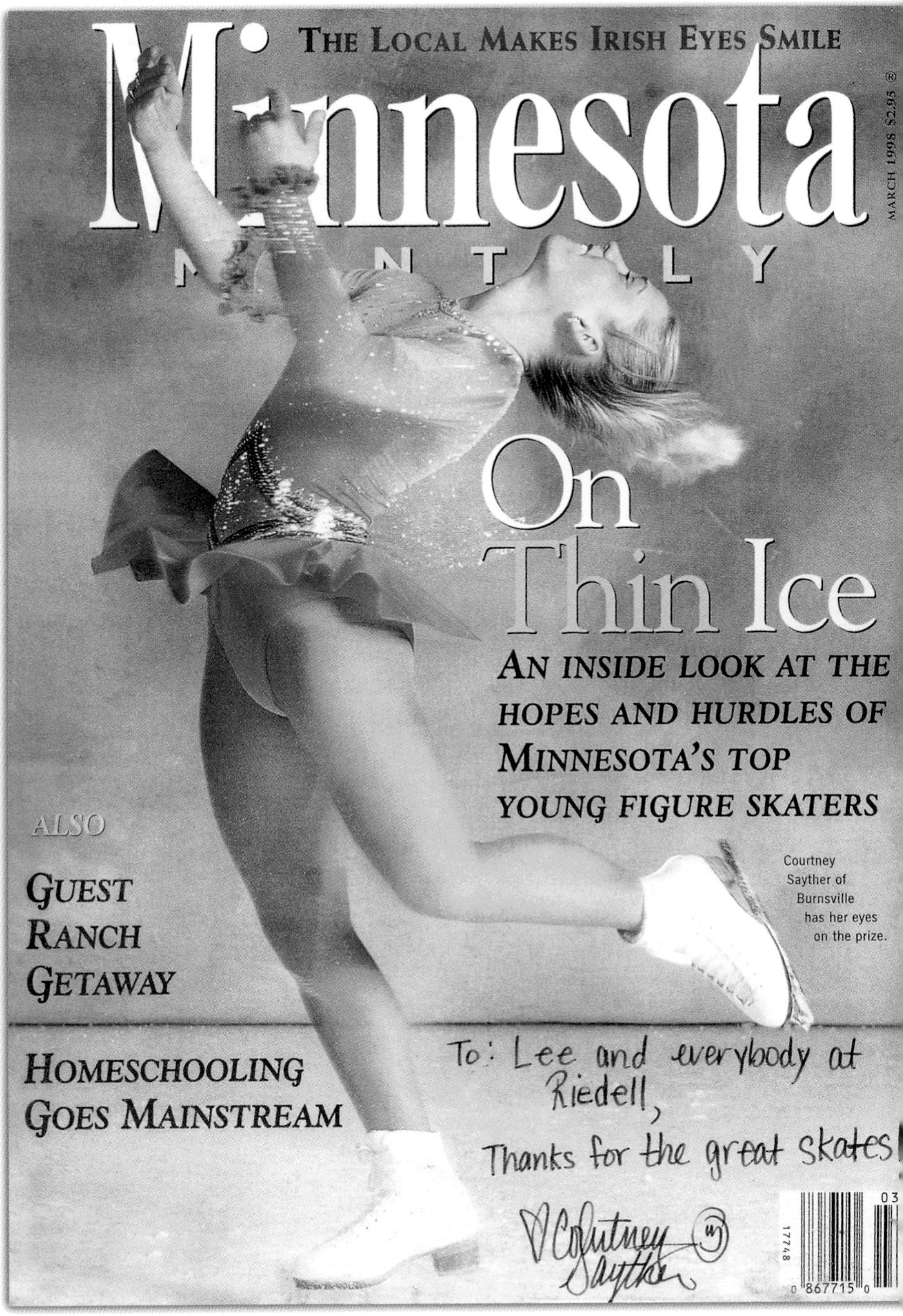

THE LOCAL MAKES IRISH EYES SMILE

Minnesota
MONTHLY

MARCH 1998 $2.95 ®

On Thin Ice

AN INSIDE LOOK AT THE HOPES AND HURDLES OF MINNESOTA'S TOP YOUNG FIGURE SKATERS

Courtney Sayther of Burnsville has her eyes on the prize.

ALSO

GUEST RANCH GETAWAY

HOMESCHOOLING GOES MAINSTREAM

To: Lee and everybody at Riedell,
Thanks for the great skates

Courtney Sayther

Courtney Sayther of the FSC of Bloomington autographed this 1998 magazine cover for the Riedell firm.

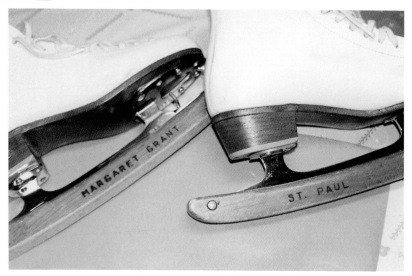

Margaret Grant Nordstog's skate blades wear their Barnard skate guards.

To protect the blades, skaters used wooden skate guards. As another St. Paul firm's ads read, the Barnard guards "fit your blades." The wooden guards had the owner's name burned into one side and the skating club name burned into the other. The guards were a Barnard invention. Sharpening the blades could be done with a machine invented by Joseph Ferrodowill of West St. Paul. A film of his work is in the collections of the Minnesota Historical Society.

From Minneapolis came a brand of tights of wool and nylon. Maribel Vinson, the nine-time women's skating champion, gave her approval to the brand called Kumfortites. They came in suntan, green, lilac, and scarlet, with a strap under the ankle. At least one copy of the advertisement accompanied an article Ms. Vinson wrote on the 1939 Nationals about to be held in St. Paul.[6]

Clothing for the recreational skater was offered through department stores, sporting goods stores such as Gokey's, and other shops. Wholesalers who read *The Dry Goods Economist* might have been tempted to order outfits modeled by "Charlotte of the Hippodrome." Their customers could skate in fashionable comfort in coats woven in shades of Copenhagen, green, old rose, canary, and white. Scarves, gloves, and Angora-trimmed hats completed the ensemble worn by the German skater in this 1915 advertisement.[7]

Newspaper testimonials bearing a photograph of a skater and his or her equipment accompanied by words of praise for the skates, blades, or boots began appearing by the 1920s. A letter written to St. Paulite

Charlotte modeled figure skating fashions in a magazine dated March 18, 1915.

Mrs. Doris Johnston, Mrs. William Rodenkirchen, Mrs. Frank Yambrick, and Mrs. Orval Murphy fashion costumes for St. Paul figure skaters like Jackie Koukal, 1957.

Raymond F. Kelly, the champion ice and roller skate racer, by the Nestor Johnson Company of Chicago illustrates the idea. The company had just sent Kelly a pair of skates and hoped to receive in return a photograph of him wearing the skates. Kelly reciprocated with a picture of himself, wearing the skates as well as a jacket covered in racing medals. The photograph appeared in the company's catalogues as well as in other advertisements.[8]

A postcard advertising the Black Forest Village at the Century of Progress, Chicago's 1934 World's Fair, showed not only the stars of its skating show—Evelyn Chandler, Beekley Miller, and Red McCarthy—but also gave an endorsement for Nestor Johnson skates.

Apparel for skaters changed, especially for those skating outdoors, as did fashions in other clothing in the 1920s. Irving Brokaw wrote that it was hard to suggest what would be appropriate, but he thought that women might wear knickerbockers to skate informally but would choose skirts for competition. A coat, ending above the knee, or a princess-style gown in black velvet he thought would do. Gone, by Brokaw's day, were the fitted jackets, ankle-length skirts, hats trimmed in fur, and fur muffs of the 1890s. Men, wrote Brokaw, wore heavy tights, leather knee-high leggings, military jackets with braid or fur trim, round hats, and white gloves.[9]

Yet, even as Brokaw wrote, what a petite Norwegian skater wore was affecting women's fashion. A photograph of the competitors in an international skating meet in the early 1920s shows Sonja Henie, then not yet a teenager, standing in a row of women. She is the youngest, the shortest, and wears a dress whose hem barely reaches her knees. It was appropriate for her age and, as other female skaters realized, easier for skaters to wear if they wanted to attempt jumps, spins, and other more athletic routines. The long, heavy skirts, like Charlotte's, were soon gone for good.[10]

An interview with Theresa Weld Blanchard, America's first national champion (in 1914), mentions some of the changes she saw in women's skating since she began competing. Women then were not supposed to do jumps, spins, or spread eagles, only "dainty little dance steps, fancy runs on our toes..." By 1941, she felt that boots were better, ice consistency had improved, and costumes allowed a skater to be more agile. Her first costume was "a frightfully snappy number, all wool, very thick, and heavy as lead. Skirts came down to the ankles. Beneath were full petticoats. And superimposing the whole was a hat about as large as a beach bonnet and twice as cumbersome." [11]

Martin Giesen's St. Paul costume house supplied costumes for the first ice skating shows at the Hippodrome and the St. Paul Auditorium Arena. Giesen, his mother Marie, and wife Olga had been the costumers for plays, operas, masquerades, pageants, and parades ever since the first Winter Carnival was held in 1886.[12] This firm, begun in 1872, closed after Olga Giesen's death in 1970.

Although there were paid dressmakers and rental costume houses such as Giesen's, skating costumes for at least some of the St. Paul Pop Concerts were "mother-made" as one skater recalled. A show's choreographer might design the appropriate wear and then the skaters' mothers took over the cutting and sewing. Janet Gerhauser Carpenter recalled making trips to Amluxen's on Nicollet Avenue in Minneapolis, to look for interesting costume fabrics. Just before the Pop Concert season began in 1949, a reporter wondered about its behind-the-scene story.

Why were the skaters' mothers working so hard to ensure their daughters' success on the ice? Since most of the women made all the solo costumes, the reporter was sure that they must work at that all night since they seemed to be rink-side all day. The answers she received were varied. They told her they were proud of the girls' achievements and thrilled when they heard the applause for the skating. Only one woman indicated a hope that her daughter would have a professional career as her aunt did in the *Ice Capades*.[13]

Costumes for Eddie Shipstad and Oscar Johnson's first performances were either rented or homemade. Oscar's sister Florence was one seamstress. Roy Shipstad took credit for stitching 16,000 spangles on the long underwear top of his early costume (now in the collection of the Minnesota Historical Society). Shipstad's costume, as seen in photographs, was improvised yet it seems remarkably modern, like the spangled body suits worn by many male skaters today.

One famous *Ice Follies* costume was found in New York City. Eddie Shipstad and Oscar Johnson had been performing their Bowery act between periods of New York Rangers hockey games at Madison Square Garden. They were a success, but the Garden manager thought his audience needed something different. He suggested that the boys should do a novelty number dressed as a horse. So they set off in search of a horse costume. The first time Eddie and Oscar, inside the horse, skated around the rink, they realized the problem. There was no way to see ahead. Suddenly they crashed through the rink boards, flattening the press box en route. After that they cut a small hole in the horse's head to see out and the skating horse became a longtime *Follies* hit.[14] Wearing a blanket with the name "Spark Plug" printed on it, their horse act was seen in St. Paul at the *Follies* produced for the benefit of the Children's Hospital Association.[15]

The Shipstad brothers and Johnson's *Ice Follies* programs often stressed the contrast between their situation at the outset and their costume needs of a decade later. On their first tour to Tulsa, on November 3, 1936, everything—props, costumes, and skaters—went in one bus. By the 1950s the *Ice Follies* traveled by train with six baggage cars to carry everything except the skaters who rode in proper passenger cars of the train.[16] Costumes in the 1940s, said Marion Curry, a former Ice Folliette, were carefully hung in huge state-of-the-art metal crates that opened from the middle of one side to the top. Each crate held costumes for four to six girls.

After the headquarters of the *Follies* moved to California, costume designers were sought from the Hollywood film industry. Helen Rose

Even a famous performer like Spark Plug of the Ice Follies *needed a bit of practice time on a St. Paul lake.*

(1904-1985) was the first to work on the *Ice Follies* costumes. She was followed in 1956 by Renie Brouillet Conley (1901-1992). What they imagined, and then was made in the *Follies* costume shop, had to withstand the rigors of use and travel. Former *Follies* skaters remember fondly the elegance of the gowns and the elaborate headgear. Often the longer dresses had semi ice-proof hems attached to the skirts, so skaters had to be careful that their skirts didn't touch the floor. Referring to the designer's work, one Folliette who skated in the show in the early 1940s exclaimed, "And if we didn't have boobs they made 'em!" Once the season ended, the costumes were not used again but were given to another ice show, the *Ice Cycles*.

The slim Folliette often skated with pounds of extra weight incorporated into her costume. One dramatic routine was skated in the dark. The skaters wore fluorescent tubes around their necks and skirts. The tubes were powered by a fifteen pound battery covered in a satin case placed flat against the skaters' backs. When the batteries failed, as they sometimes did, there would be two or three "dark" girls skating around, a former *Follies* skater remembered.[17]

Sonja Henie's affect on the costumes worn by female skaters has been mentioned, but her success in competitions, shows, and movies convinced people worldwide to take up skating. Some wanted to skate and be as graceful or athletic as she was. "When I was little we all wanted to be Sonja Henie," one friend remembers. She learned to skate on the pond in her Connecticut village. Roy Blakey, Minneapolis photographer, saw Henie's movie *Sun Valley Serenade* in his hometown of Enid, Oklahoma, and immediately wanted to skate in an ice show. It took a while, since at that time there were no ice rinks in Enid, but eventually he would tour as a skater with *Holiday on Ice*. Del Conroy had always been a speed skater until Sonja Henie's ice revue came on tour to Minneapolis. Some of her skaters came down a ramp and fell. Conroy thought that he could do better than that so he bought figure skates the next day. He skated in many local ice shows with the St. Paul FSC and in the Pop Concerts. Over sixty years later he still skates, but now with other long blade skaters at Aldrich arena. And finally, there is Dennis Kienitz. His mother was a fan of Sonja Henie and saved clippings, programs, and photographs. Kienitz inherited her scrapbook and has expanded the collection to include performance films, videos of her movies, Henie dolls, and costumes displayed on mannequins.[18] Items from Kienitz's collection illustrated an article on Sonja Henie in the 2006 tour program of *Champions on Ice*.

1.   Dorothy Snell Curtis. "Changing Edges," 5.
2.   Letter dated April 3, 1935, in Strauss Skate Company Records, Minnesota Historical Society.
3.   Ernie Pyle. *Washington Daily News*, August 14, 1941.
4.   *St. Paul Dispatch*, December 14, 1924, 1.
5.   See Fred Leighton. "Red Wing Skating Shoe Capital," *St. Paul Pioneer Press*, December 8, 1957, B1. and *Red Wing Republican Eagle*, December 8, 1997, 7.
6.   Maribel Vinson. "Can You Spot A Champion?" *Golfer and Sportsman* (January 1939), 24-26, 61.
7.   Advertisement from the *Dry Goods Economist*, December 18, 1915.
8.   Letter dated September 18, 1919, and Nestor Johnson catalogues in Raymond F. Kelly Papers, Minnesota Historical Society.
9.   Irving Brokaw. *The Art of Skating* (1926), 214-215.
10.   U.S. Figure Skating Association. *The Official History of Skating*, (1998),142.
11.   Gordon Campbell. "Former Star Notes Changes in Sport of Figure Skating," *Christian Science Monitor*, undated clipping, c. 1941.
12.   Virginia L. Martin. "A Ninety-Year Run. Giesen's: Costumers to St. Paul's Festivals and Families. 1872-1970," *Ramsey County History* 28:4 (Winter 1994), 4-15.
13.   Sally Forth. "Mother Wore Skates," *St. Paul Pioneer Press*, July 10, 1949, Women's section, 1.
14.   Oscar Johnson. *Ice Follies* program (1936), 14.

15. *St. Paul Pioneer Press*, April 8, 1934, 4.
16. *Ice Follies 20th Anniversary* program (1956), 7.
17. Misti Snow. "Fifty Years on Ice," *Minneapolis Star Tribune* Sunday Magazine, March 16, 1986, 24.
18. "Minneapolis man devotes apartment to Henie's memory," *Minneapolis Star Tribune*, January 23, 1994, 8C.

Chapter Three

Places to Skate: The Clubs and the Rinks

Skating clubs for those interested in having a regularly maintained location for their sport were established in Philadelphia (in 1849) and later in Boston and New York City. In the Twin Cities skating was more informal and less organized in nature until after 1900. The skating clubs formed at the time of the first St. Paul Winter Carnival were temporary associations. Members met to skate on available skating rinks, march in the parades, and organize parties. Only the Nushka Club outlived the carnivals. The Nushka enthusiasm for outdoor sports led to the establishment of the Town and Country Club at Marshall Avenue and the River Road in 1890. Many later members of that club participated in Winter Carnival events and the 1916 Ice Palace was built on the club grounds.

Other clubs were launched to monitor outdoor rinks. In 1901 a young boy named George Bryant, then aged ten, moved to St. Paul with his parents. The family lived in an apartment on Selby Avenue, and he attended the Neill School at Laurel and Farrington Streets. Decades later Bryant wrote several pages of reminiscences about his three years in St. Paul. The eighth section of his memoir is called "The Skating Rink," and it suggests what early outdoor rinks were like:

> Almost adjacent to the school which I attended there was a privately operated skating rink where most of the boys (and many girls) went in the afternoons after school and on Saturdays and Sundays. The rink was rather large and was well maintained; for night skaters there were a few electric lights strung around the edge of ice. At the Selby Avenue end of the rink the owner had built a frame building which served as a place to change from shoes to skates, or to buy a bit of lunch (on Saturdays). Large sandwiches were 10¢, pie was 5¢ and

Members of the Oxford Club wave to photographer John W. G. Dunn from their Grand Avenue rink, 1917. Note the Carnival costumes some children are wearing.

milk was 3¢. I presume coffee was also available.

On Saturdays, for those who remained most of the day, the lunch was anticipated with pleasure… The admission to the rink was 10¢ for one full day, but the most popular plan was to use the $3 season ticket. This rink, during my first winter in St. Paul, provided good skating for at least four months. Never had I skated so much or enjoyed it so much. Furthermore, I had my first learner's lessons in playing hockey.

Now, about the skating, I was just one of several who were told the same thing: If you're going to play hockey, you've got to concentrate on the puck and the other players (not watching your own feet every second). In an effort to correct our amateurish ways, our genial instructor [a young man who had played college hockey] put me (and others) through some lessons in pure skating—in other words, forget the hockey stick and puck for the time being. He devised practice routines for us: short dash races, four-lap races, and then some obstacle routines. First he placed a dozen barrels in a row, and had us skate through the snake-like course, until we could almost drop from exhaustion. Next, he placed some six-inch logs in a row and had us jump over these, to teach us flexibility in our skating. Well, the net result of all of this was that we *did* learn something. We played our hockey games. We had our spills, our cracks on the shins, and some satisfaction that *maybe* we might someday become fair to middlin' players.[1]

After the skating, Bryant continued, kids would toboggan on a nearby slide and then hope that another game was possible: hopping rides on the sled runners of local horse-drawn delivery wagons. Winter in St. Paul offered many possible activities.

Another early skating club was a neighborhood group attracting membership from the Grand Avenue area in St. Paul.[2] A ravine or natural depression along the south side of Grand between Oxford and Lexington had often been used by children as a hill for sledding or tobogganing. The water that collected at the bottom became a pond used for skating in the winter and floating boats in the summer. Neighbors incorporated the Oxford Club in 1916 to maintain the property and a warming house they built for sports. Stairs leading to the pond and a bandstand followed. Dues were at first five dollars per family and the membership rose to 500 people. For over a decade interest lasted, but by 1928 the club closed. The warming house and bandstand burned. Dirt was hauled in to fill the depression. Eventually Port's restaurant opened where skaters once cavorted and now an office of Edina Realty occupies the spot.

Membership card for one of St. Paul's indoor rinks.

Indoor rinks in St. Paul included the Lexington and John Davidson's rinks located approximately where the Field-Schlick store once was. Both of these rinks offered ice skating in the winter and roller skating in the summer.

Minnesota now has over forty figure skating clubs that are affiliated with the USFS. Some are members of the Twin City Figure Skating Association (see TCFSA section in this chapter). Many began during the ice rink building boom of the 1970s, although others are older. Other

Minnesota clubs include the Albert Lea FSC, Alexandria FSC, Babbitt FSC, Bemidji FSC Inc., Chisholm SC, The College of St. Scholastica (a collegiate club), Crookston FSC, Fergus Falls SC Inc., Greenway Emerald Ice (Coleraine), Hibbing FSC, International Falls FSC, Lakes FSC (Detroit Lakes), Lincoln High School FSC (a school-affiliated club), New Prague FSC, New Ulm FSC, Northern Lights FSC (East Grand Forks), Owatonna FSC, Park Rapids FSC, Riverside FSC (Austin), Star of the North SC (Grand Rapids), River Falls SC (Thief River Falls), Winona FSC, and Winter Wonderland FSC (Little Falls). Lack of space limits the discussion to only a few of the clubs, but all have contributed to the growth of the sport in Minnesota.

The Hippodrome Skating Club of St. Paul

The Hippodrome Skating Club was the first indoor skating club to be launched in the Twin Cities. The Hippodrome was built at the Minnesota State Fairgrounds in 1906. James J. Hill, the railroad tycoon and animal breeder, spoke at the dedication of the building. Three years later a club for skaters began. Officers of the club regulated ice time on what was said to be the largest indoor rink in the country (270 by 119 feet). The first Carnival was held during the club's first year of operation.

A typical mix of events is listed on the program for the seventh annual Carnival presented on February 10, 1916. Pair skaters opened the show doing spins, spirals, and whirls; they were followed by C. I. Christenson (Minnesota's national champion a decade later). Third was a race for novice

Mammoth Live Stock Pavilion, Seating 7,000, Minnesota State Fair,

View of the Hippodrome which was built in 1906 and razed forty years later at the Minnesota State Fairgrounds.

HIPPODROME ICE RINK 6
ST. PAUL - MINNEAPOLIS

LARGEST IN THE WORLD
270 x 119 FEET

Both amateur champions and future professional stars learned to skate on the Hippodrome rink.

skaters followed by a presentation of Fours skating and then Fred Premer doing fancy skating. Races then alternated with other fancy skating routines (dancing, skaters using tube skates, and two waltz contests). At the end, another mile-long race, this time for seniors, and a "plain graceful skating" contest (for club members only) took place.

The club's twenty-fifth annual Carnival in 1934 was dedicated to Gale Brooks, the co-founder, who had just died. The program featured races, comedy routines, and artistic skating by McGovern and Mack, Shirley Bowman, Phyllis Rebholz, and others.

Long after the Hippodrome closed forever, skaters remembered the hard and fast ice, and the band nights when skaters could waltz to organ music. During World War II the building became a factory for building airplane propellers and after the war ended, the Hippodrome was razed. The Coliseum, where skating also takes place, was built on the same location in 1951.

War Tax (3 cents for Men and 2 cents for Women) must be paid each time this

SEASON TICKET---1920-192

256 Hippodrome Ice Rink

Issued to *Harvey O Beck*

Address *900 Goodrich Av*

NOT TRANSFERABLE
Nct Good on Hockey or Special Attraction Nights

EYES — Male / Female / Blue / Red
HAIR — Tall / Black / Black
Medium / Brown / Brown

Many skaters belonged to more than one local club in order to have enough ice time for practice.

Arena Skating Club of Minneapolis membership card from 1930.

Minneapolis Skating Arena season ticket, signed by Lyle Wright, rink manager.

Another Minneapolis Skating Arena season ticket, signed by Lyle Wright.

The Figure Skating Club of Minneapolis

Minneapolis skaters founded two clubs, the Municipal and the Minnesota Skating Association, both before 1921. Both clubs became charter members of the United States Figure Skating Association after that organization was established in April of 1921.[3] Other Minnesota clubs would join the national group and individual Minnesotans would take part as officers of the USFSA. By the end of the decade both Minneapolis clubs had been absorbed into the Figure Skating Club of Minneapolis, incorporated in 1929. The club's longtime home was the Minneapolis Arena at Dupont Avenue and 29th Street, but prior to that the club used the facilities of the Portland Curling Rink at 29th and Portland and the Pastimes Arena (which was also a riding stable) in St. Louis Park. John Klindworth remembered that skating at the Arena was a chilly experience because they left the windows open to keep the ice frozen.

After 1931, Twin Cities skaters would often skate in the Minneapolis Arena in the winter season and then move to the St. Paul Arena for the summer. It was not a complete year-round skating experience, but it was close. Both clubs sponsored shows involving stars from elsewhere and held carnivals so there were opportunities for their own skaters to perform as well as train and practice for the tests.

Minneapolis began holding its carnivals in 1937, usually in late February or March. Directors in the early years were the teaching professionals: Joe and Ruth Gunberg, Margaret Bennett Anthony, Frances Johnson Olson, Virginia Lavelle, and Struan Complin. Stars of the carnivals were

WINTER GARDEN IN PORTLANDIA

•

PRESENTED BY

FIGURE SKATING CLUB OF MINNEAPOLIS

•

FIRST ANNUAL CARNIVAL

•

FEBRUARY 19th and 20th, 1937

Figure Skating Club of Minneapolis

Carnivals marked the season finale for many clubs. Shows were often choreographed by a club's professional coaches like Joe and Ruth Gunberg who produced the 1937 Winter Garden program. New York City was the theme of the 1984 show with the cover designed by Tom Riddle.

usually club members. As amateurs, they performed by permission from the USFSA ("sanctioned" is the term used), when the club's professionals participated. Several carnival programs proudly note that all of the cast members were recruited from the club. By the 1940s and 1950s the programs could also state with pride that those members had already won national titles as single skaters, pairs, and as Fours.

There were, of course, shows that involved invited stars. In 1930 and 1934 Sonja Henie, who had won Norwegian and world titles, and two of her Olympic set of three crowns, was asked to perform in Minneapolis. For her 1934 show, the FSC of Minneapolis and the Norwegian American Club of Minneapolis joined forces to sponsor a show at the Arena featuring not only Miss Henie but also the Norwegian Glee Club of Minneapolis singing Norwegian songs. Minnesotans liked the combination of skating with live choral and orchestral music. That mix of art forms would prove successful in the St. Paul Pop Concerts for many years.

Others in that 1934 show included Lois Dworshak and Ann Haroldson of Duluth, Robin Lee and Dorothy Snell of St. Paul, McGowan and Mack, Heinie Brock, and Margaret and Mary Simpson of Banff, Canada. Maude the Skating Donkey came to life thanks to Eddie Shipstad and Oscar Johnson and there was a Minneapolis FSC Four (three daughters of Julius Nelson and their cousin). Those who attended the show saw some of the best amateur and professional skaters the area could offer.

Sonja Henie appeared twice in FSC of Minneapolis ice skating shows. Later, the *Hollywood Ice Revue*, her own touring show, which was organized with the help of Arthur Wirtz of Chicago, played in Minneapolis in its tours of 1936 and 1938. Ms. Henie had other Minnesota connections. In her film *Second Fiddle* (1939) she was cast as a Minnesota schoolteacher who wins a talent search à la the effort to find a Scarlet O'Hara and is sent to Hollywood. The film co-starred Tyrone Power and Rudy Vallee and had a score by Irving Berlin. Her other Minnesota connection came years later when Minneapolis businessman Morris Chalfen rescued her career by offering her the lead in his European company of *Holiday on Ice*.

The FSC of Minneapolis shared the Arena with long blade skaters (who came on Sunday mornings) and hockey players until 1958. Then a new rink, designed by Elizabeth Close (the state's first female architect), opened in Golden Valley. Lyman Wakefield Jr. funded what would be called the Ice Center and later the Breck Ice Center after the private school acquired the property in 1981. Michael Kirby's ice skating school briefly operated in the Ice Center and many competitions and local ice shows were held there. In 1963 the club celebrated twenty-five years of skating carnivals with a *Silver Anniversary* show choreographed and directed by Dorothy Lewis. When

The 1971 Midwestern Championships were held at the Ice Center, then home to the FSC of Minneapolis.

Breck School decided to build a new sports facility on its campus, the Ice Center was demolished during the Spring of 2001. After that an exchange of ice rinks occurred. The St. Paul FSC left the Augsburg College Arena for the rink created in the former Milwaukee Road Depot. The St. Paul club remained there until 2004 when a new home was available in the Ramsey County rink on Pleasant Avenue in St. Paul. The FSC of Minneapolis moved to the Augsburg College rink on Riverside Avenue in 2001.

The Ice Center was used by both figure skaters and hockey players. The photographs on the postcard were taken by Gene Theslof.

One man, named as honorary chair of the 1991 U.S. Nationals, held in Minneapolis, has been considered the state's Mr. Figure Skating. Lyman E. Wakefield Jr. (1911-2001) was a skater as a child and later at Dartmouth College. He served as president of both the St. Paul and Minneapolis clubs, was a national judge for over fifty years, and the builder of the Ice Center. He held various offices on the executive committee and board of the USFS. As a skater he won national titles as a member of the first St. Paul Fours team and then earned two junior titles skating with different partners, one in pairs (1943) and the other in ice dancing (1945), while affiliated with the Skating Club of Boston. For many years he skated in local shows and in the St. Paul Pop Concerts.

There have been performances at events, like an award ceremony (called "Sketches on Skates") for employees of 3M held at the St. Paul Civic Center in 1978. Featured skaters included national champions Linda Fratianne, Tai Babilonia and Randy Gardner, Charles Tickner, the Braemarettes Precision team and the Richfield FSC's Butterflies. Both the Minneapolis and St. Paul clubs participated in ice carnivals benefiting the Optimist Clubs of each city. Minneapolis skaters were also participants in a Christmas Eve television spectacular, presented on KSTP (Channel 5).

In recent years the club has actively supported several teams of synchronized skaters, known as Syncro Panache. But before drill teams became known as precision teams and then as synchro, there were the

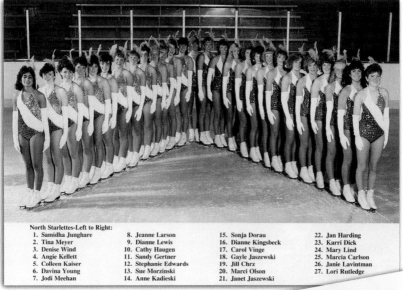

North Starlettes-Left to Right:

1. Samidha Junghare	8. Jeanne Larson	15. Sonja Dorau	22. Jan Harding
2. Tina Meyer	9. Dianne Lewis	16. Dianne Kingsbeck	23. Karri Dick
3. Denise Wind	10. Cathy Haugen	17. Carol Vinge	24. Mary Lind
4. Angie Kellett	11. Sandy Gertner	18. Gayle Jaszewski	25. Marcia Carlson
5. Colleen Kaiser	12. Stephanie Edwards	19. Jill Chrz	26. Janie Lavintman
6. Davina Young	13. Sue Morzinski	20. Marci Olson	27. Lori Rutledge
7. Jodi Meehan	14. Anne Kadieski	21. Janet Jaszewski	

The North Starlettes were one of the first precision skating teams in the metro area.

North Starlettes. This group of Minneapolis club skaters was asked to perform during the intermission of hockey games played by the Minnesota North Stars at the Met Sports Center in Bloomington. Jerre LeTourneau and Janet Hoitomt coached the North Starlettes and have continued to work with different levels of synchro skaters.

Syncro Panache teams are divided by age into Preliminary (75 percent of the skaters must be 9 or younger, 25 percent may be 11 or younger); Juvenile (under age 11); Novice (under age 14); Senior (14 and over); and Adult (over 21). In January 1990 three of the teams went to the MILK International Precision Championships in Helsinki, Finland. The Mini-Minneapplettes (the Novice team) and Minneapplettes (the Senior team) won gold medals. The Adult team skated an exhibition

PROGRAM

OHJELMA

INTERNATIONAL PRECISION SKATING COMPETITION

'90 MILK *Precision*

5.–6.1.1990
HELSINKI
FINLAND

FINNISH FIGURE SKATING ASSOCIATION

1. KANSAINVÄLINEN
MUODOSTELMALUISTELUKILPAILU
HELSINGIN JÄÄHALLISSA 5.–6.1.9
INTERNATIONAL PRECISION SKATING COMPETITIO

The FSC of Minneapolis sent three of its precision teams to this international competition.

Program for the first Children's Hospital benefit performance produced by the Shipstads and Oscar Johnson.

performance. In 1998 the Adult team won the gold medal at the U.S. National Championships. The Syncro Panache skaters have medaled in other regional and national competitions since that time. Coaches have been Janet Hoitomt and Jerre LeTourneau.

One of the charter member clubs to form the USFSA in April 1921 was the Twin City Figure Skating Club. Both C. I. Christenson and Robin Lee listed it as their home club when they won national championships: Christenson in winning the senior men's title in 1926 and Lee when he became junior men's champ in 1932. By the mid-1930s that club was gone, replaced by the two city clubs: the St. Paul FSC, incorporated in 1938, but begun earlier, and the FSC of Minneapolis, incorporated in 1929.

The St. Paul Figure Skating Club

Those who wanted to start a club in St. Paul met in Frederick Premer's home in the spring of 1935. Premer, former Hippodrome Club president, was chosen as the club's first president. The home ice for the club was the Annex or Arena added to the Auditorium in 1931 in the blocks between Seven Corners and Rice Park. The Auditorium was razed in 1982 after seventy-five years of serving the city's entertainment needs.

In the 1930s public interest in figure skating was growing rapidly. Eddie Shipstad and Oscar Johnson had discovered their calling as both a comic skating duo and as skating show producers. The St. Paul Pop Concerts were launched in 1936 and the St. Paul FSC became famous nationally because it had "summer ice," just as Lake Placid did.

Skaters rented patch time to practice their figures and expected to take part in the club's Pop Concerts. Local newspaper accounts often listed the names of skaters who had signed up for the summer sessions. One summer, pro Montgomery Wilson went on the road (an 8,000 mile trip through the Southwest) to promote the sessions and concerts.[4]

Shipstads and Johnson's *Ice Follies*, the first touring ice revue, is part of the history of theatrical skating (see Chapter Four), but what led up to that show is part of both the St. Paul and Minneapolis clubs' early history. Eddie Shipstad (1907-1998) and Oscar Johnson (1898-1970) had first skated in a show at the Hippodrome. Their comic styles matched so by the time of the Midsummer Ice Carnival, produced for the Kiwanis national convention in 1925, they were listed on the program as a "Comedy Acrobatic Act." They were soon invited to perform between periods of hockey games and asked to stage other shows. Their first local effort, held in the winter of 1933 in Minneapolis, was not a success, but other shows in St. Paul's Auditorium were. A Midsummer Carnival held on August 2, 1933, starred Evelyn Chandler, Connie Wilson, and Montgomery Wilson, all Canadian skaters. The following year Shipstad and Johnson, by now aided by Eddie's brother Roy (1910-1975), were asked to produce a benefit show for the new Children's Hospital. Fundraising events have often involved dinners, teas, luncheons, or balls. An evening of ice skating and music was different. The hospital had opened its doors in 1928 at 311 Pleasant Avenue, St. Paul, with the goal of caring for all children whether their parents could pay or not. The ice skating show proceeds went to what was called the Free Bed Fund.

Shipstad and Johnson called on their friends from the professional skating community; the Children's Hospital Association (the hospital's volunteer group) called on the Junior League of St. Paul; and both relied on the TCFSC for assistance and skaters.

Josephine McCormack, the CHA's board chair, chaired the *Ice Follies* in both 1934 and 1935. Music was provided by the WTCN Orchestra, led by Frank Zdarsky. The cast included Evelyn Chandler, Heinie Brock, Robin Lee, Ruby and Bobby Maxson, Margaret Bennett Anthony, the four Nelson sisters, and the four Leary brothers. Others who would soon be collecting their share of medals and fame were in the cast, such as Dorothy Lewis, Janette Ahrens, Margaret Grant, Bill Swallender, and Dorothy Snell. Heinie Brock skated his "Dying Duck" and barrel-jumping routines. Shipstad and Johnson donned a bull costume to be part of a bullfight and later performed their "Man on a Flying Trapeze" act.

On November 7, 1936, the Shipstads and Johnson drove off to Tulsa with a busload filled with props, costumes, and the cast of their brand new *Ice Follies* production. For the CHA, however, the ice shows had been so successful that they didn't want to curtail the idea. Working with the new St. Paul FSC, the CHA staged four more *Follies* shows, in 1936, 1937, 1938 and 1939. Professional skaters came to star and direct the shows. Local skaters had the opportunity to learn from Maribel Vinson and Montgomery Wilson as they produced the *Follies* and the new Summer Pop Concerts that followed.

For the Children's Hospital *Ice Follies* of 1938 Orrin Markhus served as director. The theme of this "Varsity Show on Skates" was college life. Ben Barnett's orchestra accompanied choral groups from Hamline University,

The cast of the 1937 Children's Hospital Ice Follies *poses. Below the "I" of the word* Follies *is child star, Irene Davidson, later to become Irene Dare in films.*

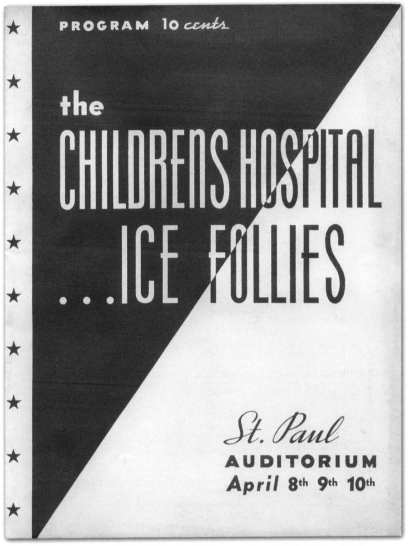

Program for the 1938 Children's Hospital Follies, *produced by the St. Paul FSC.*

the University of Minnesota, and the St. Paul Academy. Evelyn Chandler and her husband Bruce Mapes, Canadian pair champions Louise Betram and Stewart Reburn, Robin Lee, and skaters from the Winnipeg Winter Club, the Hippodrome, and St. Paul FSC all performed. One unusual number, called "Clown's Dream," included sixty-four children, Ted Cave, and Tito, a small donkey from Palermo, Sicily, pulling a hand painted cart. Prior to the *Ice Follies,* the Christian twins (Peggy and Henry) rode in Tito's cart to distribute *Follies* advertising in White Bear Lake where his owners lived.

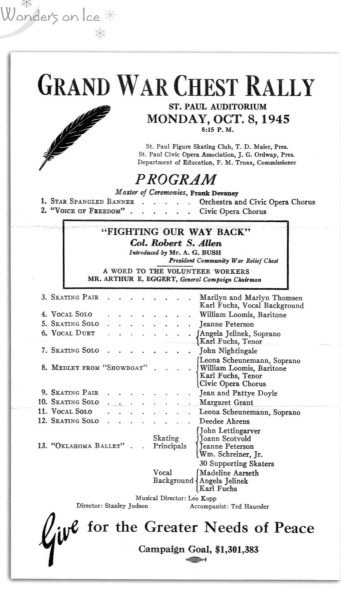

GRAND WAR CHEST RALLY

ST. PAUL AUDITORIUM
MONDAY, OCT. 8, 1945
8:15 P. M.

St. Paul Figure Skating Club, T. D. Maier, Pres.
St. Paul Civic Opera Association, J. G. Ordway, Pres.
Department of Education, F. M. Truax, Commissioner

PROGRAM

Master of Ceremonies, **Frank Devaney**

1. STAR SPANGLED BANNER	. . . . .	Orchestra and Civic Opera Chorus
2. "VOICE OF FREEDOM"	. . . . . .	Civic Opera Chorus

"FIGHTING OUR WAY BACK"
Col. Robert S. Allen
Introduced by Mr. A. G. BUSH
President Community War Relief Chest

A WORD TO THE VOLUNTEER WORKERS
MR. ARTHUR E. EGGERT, *General Campaign Chairman*

---

3. SKATING PAIR	. . . .	Marilyn and Marlyn Thomsen / Karl Fuchs, Vocal Background
4. VOCAL SOLO	. . . .	William Loomis, Baritone
5. SKATING SOLO	. . . .	Jeanne Peterson
6. VOCAL DUET	. . . .	{Angela Jelinek, Soprano / Karl Fuchs, Tenor
7. SKATING SOLO	. . . .	John Nightingale
8. MEDLEY FROM "SHOWBOAT"	. . . .	{Leona Scheunemann, Soprano / William Loomis, Baritone / Karl Fuchs, Tenor / Civic Opera Chorus
9. SKATING PAIR	. . . .	Jean and Pattye Doyle
10. SKATING SOLO	. . . .	Margaret Grant
11. VOCAL SOLO	. . . .	Leona Scheunemann, Soprano
12. SKATING SOLO	. . . .	Deedee Ahrens

13. "OKLAHOMA BALLET"	Skating Principals	{John Lettingarver / Joann Scotvold / Jeanne Peterson / Wm. Schreiner, Jr.
		30 Supporting Skaters
	Vocal Background	{Madeline Aarseth / Angela Jelinek / Karl Fuchs

Musical Director: Leo Kopp
Director: Stanley Judson   Accompanist: Ted Hauesler

Give for the Greater Needs of Peace

Campaign Goal, $1,301,383

Program for an October fundraising event involving St. Paul musical groups and the St. Paul FSC skaters directed by Stanley Judson.

The last of the Children's Hospital *Follies* produced by the St. Paul FSC was directed by Maribel Vinson and starred the nine-time ladies' national champion. Miss Vinson spent part of one year in St. Paul, directing the *Follies* as well as an *Ice Cavalcade* held in conjunction with the Winter Carnival.

A spring date (either in March or April) had been the time for the Children's Hospital Association benefit skating shows. Summer was the moment for the St. Paul Pop Concerts. Edward A. Furni, hired as manager of the Auditorium in 1936, had the idea for the Pop program, an idea born out of desperation.[5] Operating expenses for the Auditorium had created a debt of over $98,000 and costly repairs were also needed. Furni thought that the St. Paul FSC, the Civic Opera, and symphony orchestra musicians could collaborate on a show that would fill his empty building during its slow months. The first year 25,400 people attended the Pop Concerts. In 1944 attendance was 120,000 for the Pops, with customers paying 75¢ for rink side seats or 40¢ to sit in the balcony. By 1945 the Auditorium's debt was eliminated and the Pop Concerts were a fixture of St. Paul summers.[6]

When a photographer for *Holiday* magazine came to St. Paul to choose places and events to illustrate an article, an evening at the Pop Concert in the Auditorium Arena was a scene he chose. After his photograph appeared, the St. Paul FSC used a copy, with permission, to serve as the cover of their summer program.[7]

Either Cliff Reckow, Leo Kopp, or Max Metzger conducted the orchestra for many years of the summer concerts. Most of the musicians were members of the Minneapolis Symphony Orchestra. The traditional overture was often an excerpt from *Tales from the Vienna Woods*. Stanley Judson, formerly of Sadler's Wells, arrived in July 1941 to teach ballet and choreograph the skating. Some of his students remember him wearing galoshes on the ice, while others recall that he did wear skates although his gait was wobbly. Anne Klein always wanted to knock the ashes off his ever present cigarette but never dared. Vivi-Anne Hultén, who had been Judson's ballet student, came when he did to oversee the skating, as Rudolf and Elsie Angola did to work with ice dancing. A highlight of one of the summer concerts in 1941 was a performance of *Les Sylphides* with Robert Uppgren and Janette Ahrens in the main roles. One

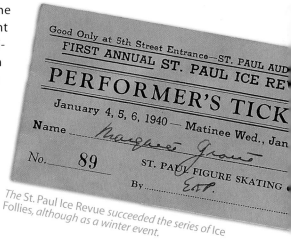

The St. Paul Ice Revue succeeded the series of Ice Follies, although as a winter event.

reporter described their skating as exquisite and not to be missed. Listed as announcer on programs for that summer was Julius Perlt, longtime voice at University of Minnesota football games.

Professional skaters arrived in the summers to coach students in the summer program and those who would participate in the Pop Concerts. Megan Taylor, Montgomery Wilson, and Maribel Vinson were among the club's early coaches. Pierre Brunet and Andrée Joly came in 1940, Robert and Joan Ogilvie in 1957. Listed in later Pop Concert programs are the names of Mary Lou Gerebi (1971), Dorothy Lewis and Barbara Hartwig Castaneda (1974), and Nate Alden and Jerre Sweno (1977) as skating directors. The last show mentioned honored that year's Winter Carnival royalty. By the 1970s the club only presented a few evening Pop Concerts each summer, but still presented them with the full complement of skaters and music performed by an orchestra. John Harvey commented that the show still offered a lot of fine skating with good costumes and a seventeen-piece orchestra with a big band sound. While he missed the stars of past Pop Concerts, he thought the soloists were more accomplished at a younger age and more "show-wise."[8]

St. Paul FSC brochure listed its coaches, schedule for patch sessions, and the opportunities for skaters to take part in the Pop Concerts.

FABULOUS MUSICAL ICE REVUE

ST. PAUL'S ORIGINAL

SAINT PAUL AUDITORIUM

Refreshments at Tables

27th Sparkling Season

The o...
s...
Upper Mi...
beaut...
da...

POP Musical ICE REVUE

27th SUMMER N...
ST. PAUL "POP" N...
July 12 Thru Aug. 24 •

Two postcards advertising the St. Paul FSC's Pop Musical Ice Revues. The 1960 card shows Margaret Grant soaring in the air, while the 1963 card uses a design borrowed from the Ice Follies program of 1954 (see page 110).

POP Musical ICE REVUE 24th SUMMER

ST. PAUL'S ORIGINAL and FABULOUS ICE SKATING REVUE ORCHESTRA of 55—SINGING

SAINT PAUL AUDITORIUM

Refreshments at Tables

Opens Friday July 8, 1960 Every Wednesday Friday & Saturday Thru September 3, 1960 8:30 P.M.

New Program Each Night

Newspaper critics James Gray, Frances Boardman, and John H. Harvey usually reported on both the skating and the music presented at the Pop Concerts. They mentioned local skaters who often appeared as well as the occasional visiting skating star. Referring to the first St. Paul Four (Mary Louise Premer, Janette Ahrens, Lyman Wakefield Jr. and Bob Uppgren), Harvey wrote that "they did the routine for which they have become famous, and did it with careless perfection." Then he described the skating of another national champion, Margaret Grant, saying that her performance "was not only spectacular but a thing of beauty in its grace and rhythmic perfection. There was a continuous flow of motion into which every gesture and figure was fitted without a break or falter. It was music on ice."[9]

The second St. Paul Fours team: Marilyn and Marlyn Thomsen, Janet Gerhauser and John Nightingale.

Above: The first St. Paul Fours team: Janette Ahrens and Robert Uppgren, Mary Louise Premer and Lyman E. Wakefield Jr.

Right: Margaret Grant, a frequent Pop Concert soloist.

Left: Del Conroy and Donna Nordhal formed one of the St. Paul FSC's adagio pairs in Pop Concerts.

Right: Taking a bow for a St. Paul FSC Pop Concert in 1962 is Barbara Hartwig.

Bobby Mecay's comedy routines were a staple of Pop Concert programs.

Looking back on twenty years of summer shows, Gareth Hiebert, the Oliver Towne columnist for the St. Paul papers, described the concerts this way:

> It was hot that July night in 1936. Gripped by the heat and the depression, the city moped in the doldrums.
>
> Maybe it was curiosity, or the "Cool" sign, or the price. But quite a few hundred came down to the St. Paul Auditorium that night to attend the premiere of what had been billed as a new kind of show.
>
> They called it the "Pop" concert in the ads.
>
> Just after 8:15 pm, the lights went up over the

St. Paul FSC skaters honored the 50th anniversary of the U.S. Air Force in 1957. Left to right are Mary Beth Tonskemper, Gay Steindorf, Martha Berg, Joan Santo, Paula Donald, and Barbara Hartwig.

sheet of blue white arena ice that sent cool vapors into the tiers of tables where, in shirt-sleeves, folks sat eating popcorn, drinking pop. The massive stage brightened.

Leo Kopp's baton fell and the bows of two dozen violins moved in unison into the lilting melody of the "Merry Widow Waltz." In the background came the voices from the Civic Opera chorus.

Out of the wings, gliding in time, moved the skaters. . . . .

In an era of waning live legitimate theater, giving way to TV productions, movies, the St. Paul Pop Musical Ice Revue remains a place where thousands of Minnesotans can, fortunately, still see what a live orchestra looks like and a line of some of the world's famed figure skaters as well as a complete opera chorus.

For, as Ed Furni says, "It began as a show for everyone; it still is a show for the people and by the people."

Because if the cost at the box office is slight, the gratuity paid the performers is less. Except for the orchestra, director and a few professional singers, skaters and production chiefs, nobody gets paid.[10]

Joan Santo and Jack Woodstrom of the St. Paul FSC photographed during the Pop Concert season of 1961.

The name of the summer series became the *St. Paul Pop Musical Ice Revue* in 1957. The last summer Pops season was held in 1977. The Pop Concerts had had an extraordinary run. When they began they were unique. No other city offered the same combination of elite amateur skating, professional singers, and a live symphony orchestra in thrice-weekly concerts at an affordable price from July until September. By the late 1960s there was more competition for dollars spent on entertainment so the highlight of so many St. Paul summers ended. In 1986 alumni of the Pop Concerts and current members of the St. Paul FSC staged a 50th anniversary show called *The Pops One More Time*.

In the winters, skaters from the St. Paul FSC took part in St. Paul's Winter Carnivals in the *Ice Cavalcades* and in informal demonstrations on outdoor rinks held elsewhere. An undated letter from the Show Committee of the St. Paul FSC sought to arrange such appearances. It began, "Is your Community planning a carnival this year?" Any community that replied in the affirmative could expect two dozen to thirty skaters and six to eight chaperones to arrive by bus or cars. The troupe often made the trip from St. Paul, performed afternoon and evening shows, and then returned home the same evening. Clippings note ice show performances in Pipestone at the quarry rink on January 23, 1954; on Lake Winona for Winona's winter fest on January 22, 1956; in Eveleth (January 19, 1953); Rhinelander (February 20-21, 1954); and Waseca (January 18-20, 1957, and January 19, 1958).

A form letter sent to the skaters going on one of these trips cautioned them to bring tights and perhaps a cardigan sweater to wear over a costume as they would be skating outdoors and it was January. The letter concluded, "Bear in mind that the paid admissions pay our expenses. Give a good performance." Both Del Conroy and Margaret Grant remember the trips, the camaraderie, and, sometimes, the uneven quality of natural ice that made jumps and lifts dangerous.

Since 1909, when the Hippodrome FSC opened, every skating club seems to have moved at least once. Buildings have been demolished or better facilities constructed. A building known as an auditorium, arena, or center is almost always intended as a multi-purpose structure with hockey teams and figure skaters scheduling time when trade shows or concerts haven't booked the space. The Ice Center in Golden Valley (at 5800 Wayzata Boulevard) was the first building to be erected primarily for skating and the old Milwaukee Road Depot in downtown Minneapolis is the most unusual structure ever to house a rink.

The St. Paul FSC used the rinks at Aldrich arena in Maplewood and Wakota arena in South St. Paul; then moved to the Augsburg College arena at 2323 Riverside Avenue in Minneapolis. After the old railroad depot had been partially turned into an ice skating rink, the St. Paul FSC moved its activities there, staying until 2004.[11] Then the opportunity came to return to St. Paul and the Ramsey County rink on Pleasant Avenue. This arena offers one sheet of ice, but has practice rooms for other classes. St. Paul's emphasis on training the elite level skater is manifested in the success of Eliot Halverson and Rhiana Brammeier in national competition. Both won national novice titles in 2006. Eliot then repeated John Lettengarver's accomplishment of sixty years prior by then winning the national junior crown in 2007. That emphasis can be traced back to the club's first gold medalists. From the list of thirty skaters in the country who had passed their final tests by 1943, six were from St. Paul. They were Robin Lee, Mary Louise Premer, her brother Robert Premer, Arthur Preusch Jr., Janette Ahrens, and Margaret Grant.[12]

One of the most decorated skaters for the St. Paul FSC was Janette Ahrens who medaled between 1941 and 1947, when she retired. In her last national competition, when she won a silver medal in the senior ladies' event at the U.S. Nationals, she was awarded the Oscar Richards Trophy for the most artistic skating.

The Duluth Figure Skating Club

In the Twin Cities or Red Wing, Winona or Lake City, skaters could clear a stretch of river ice and have a rink. In a town near a lake or pond, that smaller space could offer winter fun. Duluth, on the shores of the greatest of the Great Lakes, built a figure skating, curling, and hockey club within sight of the water, but perhaps a few intrepid souls did try skating on Lake Superior. Outdoors, a pleasant skating experience depended on the depth of ice and whether the skin of Superior had taken shape on a wind and debris free day. Ginny Frazer Johnson remembers her father telling of testing Superior's ice by skating from Duluth to Two Harbors.

From 1924 until 1966, the place to skate was upstairs at the Duluth Figure Skating and Curling Club, a brick-over-concrete building at 1325 London Road. Downstairs was the hockey domain; upstairs was reserved for figure skating and curling. There were quiet times at the rink for patch practice and, on Sundays, a list of dances to learn. Mrs. Bunny Robb taught the dances. Jumping and spinning were not permitted during dance time. Skaters were expected to focus on the dances whose names Mrs. Robb had posted on the rink fence. Ginny Johnson, whose family lived nearby, tells of long afternoons of skating and then, when she saw the front porch lights blinking, of heading home for dinner.

22nd Annual

ICE FOLLIES

Sponsor

Duluth Figure Skating Club, Inc.

Member ... United States Figure Skating Association

Feb. 8, 9, 10, 1946

Friday, Saturday, Sunday Evenings, 8:15

Matinee Sunday 3:00

Duluth Curling & Skating Club

The Duluth FSC's Ice Follies were a vital part of Duluth's winter entertainment calendar for over forty years.

These cowgirls skated in the Duluth club's Ice Follies *of 1963. Left to right are Pat Kusch, Lisa McLean, Mary Ann Sturm, Linda Broman, Marilyn Turnquist, Julie Kurtovich, and Candy McGiffert.*

The Duluth club began with twenty-five members in 1924 and held its first *Ice Follies* that year. For many years the *Follies* sold out an entire weekend of performances (three evening and two matinee shows), but once the club moved to the new Duluth Entertainment and Convention Center it became harder to attract audiences. There was more competition for the skating entertainment dollar from Bulldog hockey games and the rehearsals of the *Ice Capades* (held in Duluth from the 1970s until 1993). So the *Ice Follies* came to an end in 1965 and the club began sponsoring the Northland non-qualifying competitions in 1980. The old clubhouse was demolished in 1985 and replaced by the city's rose garden.

During the *Follies'* long run, many firm friendships were made. "It was like a family," Barb Hemmerling Thomson said. "Through skating you met your best friends. Even if you hadn't seen someone for eighteen years, you'd grab each other around the neck and it's as if you'd never been separated." In 1998 several former *Follies* skaters decided to hold a reunion at the Northland Country Club. Skaters from across the country came to remember events, look at old photos and costumes, and share the history. [13]

The club's skaters filled the *Follies* casts and took on the solos, but, as happened elsewhere, there were guest stars: Jimmy Waldo, Barbara Hartwig and Bobby Mecay, the St. Paul Fours, and even a ten-year-old Janet Lynn who skated in a Cinderella's Ball scene in 1964. In the very earliest shows, skaters were those who would go on to professional stardom like Lois Dworshak and Ann Haroldson. Productions were planned and choreographed by the club pros: Mimi Pong Page, Norton Wait, Alec McGowan, and Bob O'Connell are listed on program pages.

Programs also indicate the change that took place in musical material. Club ice shows used music often drawn from the ballet world in the 1930s. Broadway and popular music were the source by the 1950s. Sugar plum fairies were replaced by Oklahoma cowgirls or the New York chorines of *Guys and Dolls*. Certainly, too, in planning programs show directors must often have been inspired by what they saw in the touring shows, even if they could not afford quite as lavish lighting, painted ice, or costumes.

Bobby Specht, from Superior, Wisconsin, skated in Duluth ice carnivals and was an Ice Capades *star for many years.*

The 1955 Duluth Ice Follies program cover shows the Aerial Lift Bridge, the Club and its popular activities: curling, figure skating, and hockey. Show director was Mimi Pong Page.

Duluth figure skaters Susan Sebo and brother-sister pair skaters, Barbara and Bruce Hemmerling, circa 1964.

The Duluth FSC has been a member of the USFS since 1927, has offered classes, and testing programs. Among its earliest gold medal winners are Barbara Hemmerling, Susan Jacobson, Zoe Peterson, John Thorson, Susan Sebo, John Hendrickson, Arlene Hildebrandt, and Bob James. Two of its current members, Angie Lien and Molly Oberstar, have been frequent competitors at regional, national, and international events.

Molly Oberstar, of the Duluth FSC has won both junior and senior Minnesota championships, medaled in regional competitions, and placed fifth in the Junior Grand Prix of Zagreb in 2005.

The Rochester Figure Skating Club

Skaters in Rochester used the city's outdoor rinks until March 9, 1939, when the Mayo Civic Auditorium was built on land given to the city by Drs. William and Charles Mayo. The auditorium offered an ice sheet measuring 85 by 150 feet, but as Carole Shulman noted, "hockey and figure skating are naturally enemies"— both groups needed to use the ice, so scheduling became a problem. Usually the ice rink could not be used from late August until October. The auditorium was the place for many other civic events so the struggle for ice time by the skaters was constant.

The Rochester FSC was organized in 1939 after the opening of the auditorium and incorporated on March 20, 1940, by Drs. C. K. Maytum and E. L. Foss and Miss Mabelle Dilley. Dedication ceremonies for the auditorium involved skaters from the St. Paul FSC. Pleased with its new facility, the city celebrated again one year later. A large crowd watched programs by the Rochester Symphony and Choral Society in the theater, dancing in the North Hall, and skating in the arena. Members of the Rochester FSC performed a ballet, both junior and senior fours teams did routines, and the headliner was Margaret Grant of St. Paul who had won national silver and bronze medals by age eleven. Miss Grant's solo included "many advanced figures and she was presented with a sheaf of roses."[14]

At first the club's founders stressed "skating for fun," but by the summer members were participating in Pop Concerts thrice weekly directed by Dorothy Franey, the speed skater. Like the St. Paul Pop Concerts, the *Skate Parades* used a live orchestra, led by Orvis Ross or Harry Strobel, and featured members of the city's symphony.

The musical program for the skaters in 1941 was a combination of classical waltzes, Gershwin's "Strike Up the Band," and the Andrews Sisters' "Scrub Me, Mama, with a Boogie Beat." In 1943 Dorothy Snell, visiting pro, changed the format by using almost all of the club's two-hundred members in ice ballets based on *Hansel and Gretel* and *Tales from the Vienna Woods*. Gretchen Wilson, now a piano teacher as well as a figure skating judge, remembers being one of four skaters in Bach's Fugue in G Minor in the *Skate Parade* of 1960.[15] Helen Uhl Black directed the foursome to respond to the voices in Bach's composition, choreography that Ms. Wilson found delightful.

With the availability of summer ice, Rochester attracted elite skaters and coaches who wanted the practice time. *Ice Follies* cast members on vacation also came to Rochester to skate. The club hired a professional coach, Struan Complin, both to teach and stage a show. Complin, a Canadian, was also a part-time coach for the FSC of Minneapolis. The first *Skate Parade* was held on April 12-13, 1940. Later shows featured St. Paul

Above: "A Bit O' Scotch", directed by Carole Shulman, was a featured number in the Rochester FSC's Skate Parade of 1967.

Skate Parade

PRESENTED BY

ROCHESTER FIGURE SKATING CLUB, INC.

APRIL 1-2, 1943

MAYO CIVIC AUDITORIUM

Right: Dorothy Snell, then visiting pro, choreographed the Rochester FSC's Skate Parade in 1943.

skaters Mary Louise Premer and Janette Ahrens, Canadian champion Mary Rose Thacker[16], Wisconsin's Bobby Specht, and the *Ice Follies* comic Heinie Brock. Over the years other professional skaters including Dorothy Snell, Rudolf and Elsie Angola, Megan Taylor, Winnie Silverthorne, Helen Uhl Black, Richard Vraa, Charlie Murphy, and Barbara Kossowska (from Poland) would spend a season or more coaching in Rochester. Carole and David Shulman came in 1963 to take up duties as coaches; Carole retired from coaching in 1977 and from the club in 1984.

In 1975 the club moved to a new facility, the Rochester-Olmsted County Recreation Center at 31 Elton Hills Drive N.W. Two ice sheets were part of the building—one for hockey (85 by 200 feet), one for skating or curling (85 by 150 feet). The complaint expressed by one mother years earlier could now be answered. Speaking of the auditorium, she had said, "We need a year-round rink here. We have a Civic Theater, and an Art Center. As is, we have good potential for competitive skaters, but with the limited practice time, which must include sharing the auditorium with wrestlers, boxers, hockey players and basketball players, good skaters do not have a chance to develop."[17]

DEDICATION OF ROCHESTER-OLMSTED RECREATION CENTER

2:00 p.m.
SUNDAY, FEBRUARY 23, 1975

The Architectural Design Center of Rochester designed this multi-purpose facility with a gymnasium and space for skating, curling, hockey, and swimming.

Two of the Rochester FSC's skaters who competed successfully on the regional and national level are Beth Ann Carolin (left) and Joan Orvis (below).

Many Rochester skaters have passed their gold medal tests, beginning with Marilyn Prickman in 1954. Gold medalists Beth Ann Carolin, Joan Orvis, and Jannat Thompson competed successfully on the regional and national levels. Cathie Comartin, Eileen Kaese, Penny Johnson, Kent Orwoll, and Ms. Orvis completed their competitive seasons and joined the casts of either the *Ice Follies*, *Ice Capades*, or *Disney on Ice*. As Joan Orvis said when she joined the *Ice Follies* five days after graduating from high school, "Now I'm just tired of competition. I worked at it for four years and I'm through with it. But I didn't want all that training to go down the drain."[18] After two years with the *Follies*, she returned to Rochester and became a figure skating coach. She is now the head professional on the staff of the Braemar-City of Lakes FSC.

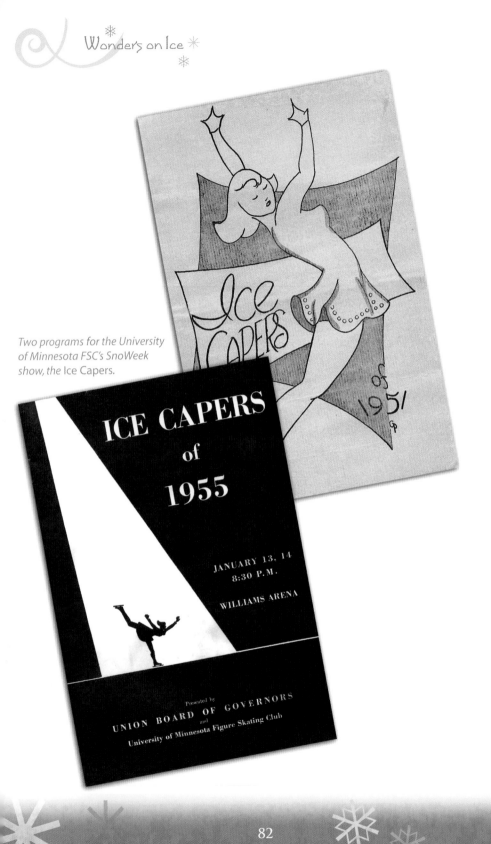

Two programs for the University of Minnesota FSC's SnoWeek show, the Ice Capers.

Ice Capers of 1951

ICE CAPERS
of
1955

JANUARY 13, 14
8:30 P.M.

WILLIAMS ARENA

Presented by

UNION BOARD OF GOVERNORS
and
University of Minnesota Figure Skating Club

University of Minnesota Figure Skating Club

In 1940 students at the University of Minnesota-Minneapolis organized a figure skating club that was recognized by the University Senate Committee of Student Affairs.[19] Students, alumni, and faculty members could join and the membership list rose to over forty at first. Then interest waned and the club went inactive until after World War II ended. Early presidents included Rudolf Gruelich, Cherry Cedarleaf, and Joyce Maul.

Usually club members came to skate on Tuesday and Thursday evenings and Sunday mornings. Some members did exhibition skating between periods of Gopher hockey games. In 1946 the winter quarter SnoWeek was revived. Among the festivities were a sleigh ride, a dogsled race, and a SnoBall presided over by a king and queen. Margaret Grant, already well known as a skater, was selected as queen and her consort was Peter Aurness, better known later as Peter Graves in his role in television's *Mission Impossible*.

Later SnoWeeks included an ice show called *Ice Capers* arranged by members of the club. By 1949 Williams Arena, the university fieldhouse, had been extensively remodeled. The west end housed hockey (or figure skating) and the east end was for basketball. The annual *Ice Capers* shows were presented at Williams Arena.

What a SnoWeek could not always rely on was pristine, newly-fallen snow. In 1951 the yearbook reported that the dance in Coffman Memorial Union, the SnoBall, had been decorated with multicolored snowflakes even though students knew that the color of snow in Minnesota was grey. Then the reporter continued, "The affair which pushed SnoWeek out of the red for the first time in several years (net profit: $1.98) was the *Ice Capers* show in Williams arena. It was a 'sell-out' crowd of 3,000."[20]

Janet Gerhauser was club president, test chair, and directed two of the *Ice Capers* shows. In 1952 Mary Louise Premer was the club's faculty advisor. Other well-known skaters who belonged to the club and performed in the ice shows were Del Conroy, Sharon Kulenkamp, Betsy Lohn, Bobby Mecay, Bud Zats, Richard Branvold, Joan Zazulak, and Neil Waldo.

Unusual for university clubs, the figure skating group was affiliated with a national group, the USFSA. Mary Louise Premer guided the club to that link and served as the USFSA chair for collegiate skating. Currently the University of Minnesota FSC is designated as a collegiate chapter and has a focus on synchronized skating.

Mariucci Arena, named for the university's famous hockey coach, replaced Williams Arena as the home for men's hockey in 1993. The first world synchro championship was held at Mariucci in 2000. Just west of Mariucci is the Ridder Arena where the university's national champion women's hockey team plays. Kathleen and Bob Ridder had long been involved in hockey and figure skating; both had become skating judges.

Among the skaters in this 1960 show were Del Conroy, Lynn Dwyer, Connie Brenner, Dawn Carlson, Lona Fai and Bona Dai Beckstrom, Barbara Hartwig and Bobby Mecay, and Jack Woodstrom.

Braemar-City of Lakes Figure Skating Club of Edina

As its name indicates, the Braemar-City of Lakes FSC had two origins. As the City of Lakes FSC, the club began at the Minneapolis Arena in 1959. When that building was wrecked, some of its skaters headed to the new Braemar Arena at 7501 Ikola Way in Edina where another club existed. Braemar originally offered one ice sheet. Now it has three, two Zambonis, and an active program in synchronized skating, which used to be called precision skating.

The first head of the new coaching staff was Eleanor Wilson Fisher, a former Canadian junior champion. Mrs. Fisher coached thirty-two skaters who passed their gold level tests. A trophy named in her honor lists these skaters and the many others who have achieved the ranking since. Eleanor Fisher teamed with Jean Pastor to launch the club's skating school in 1965. Ms. Pastor came from a speed skating family, had been active with local skating clubs, and skated with her twin sister Joan in the *Ice Follies*.

Eleanor Fisher and Jean Pastor had worked together at the Aldrich Arena, producing their first ice revue there in 1963. It grew each year, using in its casts local talented skaters and many of the three hundred students

Tamie Klindworth and her family were founding members of the Braemar-City of Lakes FSC. Now Tamie K. Campbell, she has retained her interest in the sport through judging and many other volunteer assignments.

The Team Braemar Junior Synchronized Skating Team won the gold medal at the 2006 and 2007 Midwestern Championships. They are coached by Toni Swiggum and her daughter, Pam May.

in the skating school. They produced their last show for Aldrich a week after the first show, the Braemar *Ice Frolics*, they planned for the City of Lakes FSC in April 1966. The next year, when Vivi-Anne Hultén returned to St. Paul, she opened her Fun and Pleasure Skating School at Aldrich and would direct the spring shows from then on.

The Braemar-City of Lakes FSC, like the FSC of Minneapolis, has taken a strong interest in synchro skating. The Braemarettes and now Team Braemar have medaled in a number of competitions. They are coached by Toni Swiggum, Pam May, and Jean Pastor.

Early in the club's history, a sad event showed the strength and compassion of the skating community. At the annual season-ending skating show, one skater—a well-regarded longtime skating instructor— finished his portion of the Swing Waltz, said he didn't feel well, and died. The club immediately decided to stage a benefit to raise funds for the family of the skater and teacher, Jack Woodstrom. He died on April 18, 1970; the Jack Woodstrom Benefit Ice Show took place on May 13th. Janet Lynn, the 1970 senior ladies national champion, starred in the show. The owner of the *Ice Follies*, Tom Scallen, authorized the participation of three *Follies* skaters (Jill Shipstad, Suzie Berens, and Richard Dwyer) and had a collection of *Ice Follies* costumes shipped to Edina for the event. The elegant dresses and hats were worn by *Ice Follies* alumnae, the Ex-Folliettes, who skated in the show. Bill Goldsworthy, Lou Nanne, and J.B.

The junior Team Braemar does a mass of Biellmann spins on their way to winning the gold medal at the 2007 Zagreb Snowflake competition.

Parise of the Minnesota North Stars hockey team and Roundhouse Rodney (Lynn Dwyer) of WTCN-TV took part as did skaters from the Minneapolis, St. Paul, and Braemar clubs.

Braemar singles skaters have compiled significant records. Alice Sue Claeys' family moved to Minnesota so that she could study with Ann and Mark Militano. Ms. Claeys won the U.S. national junior title in 1990[21]; she later skated with the Belgian national team in the Olympics. Kathleen

Schmelz-Gazich won national medals as a professional skater after touring with *Disney on Ice*. She is now a member of the Braemar coaching staff. Tamie Klindworth Campbell's family helped found the Braemar-City of Lakes FSC. After her competition days were over she became a judge, team leader, and is currently an officer of the USFS. Vicky Fisher Binner was named to the U.S. World Team and later coached at the club.

Twin City Figure Skating Association

Members of three of the local skating clubs—St. Paul, Minneapolis, and Braemar—worked on the 1973 U.S. Nationals held at the Met Sports Center in Bloomington. As a direct result of that experience and using the $20,000 earned as profits, John Klindworth, Matthew Zats, Gil Holmes, and Richard Klein decided to form an umbrella or interclub group, called the Twin City Figure Skating Association (TCFSA). The purpose of the group, according to its by-laws, is to "foster, promote, improve, and encourage the sport of figure skating among youth under 18 years of age in the State of Minnesota, to promote cooperation between the member clubs and to encourage and facilitate participation in regional, sectional, national, and international figure skating competitions."

Three clubs became the charter members of the TCFSA; total number of clubs as members is now several times that.[22] Having such a group would provide ease of communication and mechanisms for sharing the workload of tests, local championships, and national events. TCFSA's sponsorship of major events continues through the U.S. Nationals of 2008. Presidents of the TCFSA have been Richard Klein, Elizabeth Harty, Pat St. Peter, Bette Snuggerud, Merry Fragomeni, Marlys Larson, William Wiles, John Klindworth, Gil Holmes, Don Pilarski, Jeanne Wind, and currently, Lynda Lubratt. A publication called *Rink Link*, published three times annually and edited by Lexie Kastner, is sent to the members of the clubs.

As former TCFSA president Bette Snuggerud said, having a group such as the TCFSA is unusual in the skating world. "In other places clubs compete for members," she explained. "Here we work together. Our goal was to host every kind of event possible that the United States Figure Skating Association sponsored. We would be the local expertise or energy, and would supply the many volunteers necessary to staff these events."[23] Since 1980 the TCFSA has sponsored the Minnesota State Championships held first in the Spring and now in August. This is a non-qualifying event that, like other similar competitions, offers experience to eligible skaters. Winners of the competition are listed in the Appendix.

In 1976 (with *America and Its Music*) and 1977 (*It's A Wonderful World*), the TCFSA's eleven member clubs staged benefit ice shows to aid the Hennepin County Chapter of the American Lung Association and the USFSA's Memorial Fund. The cast featured national champions Tai Babilonia, Randy Gardner, David Santee, and Janet Lynn (in 1976), and Linda Fratianne (in 1977). Each club contributed a number of its skaters. Maplewood and Braemar used their precision teams; Richfield sent its Butterflies, a group of skaters who used long fabric wings in their routine. The first year, some of the Ex-Folliettes skated and both years Ritter Shumway and Harlene Lee led a group of local pros in a Swing Waltz.

The TCFSA awards a number of prizes at its annual banquet. A prize given to the senior female skater with the best academic and placement record at the State Championship is named for Bette Snuggerud. An equivalent award is given to a male skater in memory of James Disbrow, chair of the 1998 World Championships. The synchro team with the highest competitive achievement is given an award in the name of Marlys Larson and the club with the best record in competition receives honors named for Lyman Wakefield Jr. and his daughter, Louise Wakefield.

Another award is bestowed each year on a TCFSA volunteer. It honors service to the sport by someone who is a Minnesotan and a member of one of the clubs. Since 1993 this honor, The Champion in Figure Skating Award, has been given to Marlys Larson, Bette Snuggerud, Beverly Arneson, Janet Carpenter, Lexie Kastner, Merry Fragomeni, Sylvia Olson, Jimmy Disbrow, Lynda Lubratt, Anne Klein, Carolyn Marker, Chip Rauth, Pat St. Peter, and Shirley Hage.

Many of the same national stars and talented local skaters appeared in a benefit performance TCFSA arranged for the St. Paul Chamber Orchestra at the St. Paul Civic Center in 1984. The evening was called *Champions on Ice*. Tai Babilonia and Randy Gardner, Toller Cranston, Richard Dwyer (the second "Mr. Debonair" of the *Ice Follies*, succeeding Roy Shipstad), and the duo of Ritter Shumway and Harlene Lee headed the program. Member clubs sent their precision lines to perform, including the Minneapplettes, the North Starlettes, the Braemarettes, the Lake Minnetonka teams, and the Richfield Butterflies.

In addition to benefit performances, TCFSA, its clubs, and members have served on the local organizing committees for the 1991 U.S. Nationals, the 1998 Worlds, the 2000 World Precision Championship, and the 2008 Nationals (See Chapter 6 for a list of all these events).

An opening ceremony often sets the tone for an event. The excitement, anticipation, and importance of what is to come can be emphasized in the choreography. TCFSA was asked to provide a precision team for the opening of the 1980 Winter Olympics at Lake Placid. The skaters came from several clubs and were proud of the chance to present this form of skating to a worldwide audience.

In 1985 a very different number inaugurated the *Skate America* competition at the St. Paul Civic Center. Nineteen nations sent skaters to compete in the senior singles, pairs, and ice dancing events. To honor those countries nineteen pairs of local skaters were costumed in the national dress of the countries and given appropriate flags to carry as they skated to "We Are the World."

Three years later the TCFSA undertook a Command Performance for King Carl XVI Gustaf and Queen Silvia of Sweden. The Swedish royal pair was in the United States for events in connection with a yearlong commemoration of the 350th anniversary of the first Swedish settlement in America. *New Sweden '88* included art exhibits and concerts and an ice extravaganza at the Met Sports

Two of the skaters in the "We Are the World" opening ceremonies for Skate America in 1985.

Ticket for the
New Sweden Ice Skating
Extravaganza, *1988.*

Center in Bloomington on April 24, 1988. Harriet Sutton Hield was director and choreographer for the show. Stars were Canadian national champion Brian Pockar, American dance champions Judy Blumberg and Michael Seibert, Peggy Fleming, Rosalyn Sumners, Robin Cousins, and the 1987 Swedish national champions Lotta Falkenbach and Peter Johansson. Music was provided by the Gustavus Adolphus College Choir, Band, and Herald Trumpeters. From the local skating community those who had recently participated in the U.S. Nationals were chosen (Lisa Cornelius, Stephanie Hillstrom, Robyn Petroskey, Gig Siruno, Davin Grindstaff, and Kathryn Curielli). The Minneapplettes and the Lake Minnetonka precision lines skated. One number, called "A Salute to Sweden," featured Vivi-Anne Hultén. She was delighted when the king told her he remembered seeing her skate in Sweden.

The Minnesota Skating Scholarship

Just as the TCFSA came into existence as a result of the collaboration of members of three figure skating clubs in organizing the 1973 U.S. Nationals, the Minnesota Skating Scholarship traces its birth to the next time the championships were held in Minnesota. A Skaters' Reunion was planned to welcome those who were coming to Minneapolis in 1991. An invitation announcing the party on February 14, 1991, appeared in the event program. The evening of fellowship at the Calhoun Beach Hotel launched a program of scholarships to support deserving skaters. It was announced that 10 percent of the funds raised would be contributed to the USFSA Memorial Fund; the other 90 percent would remain in Minnesota to be allocated according to guidelines established by an Advisory Board. The organizing committee was headed by Mary Wright

Richardson. The current chair is Herb Mergenthaler. After the death of Harris Collins, a member of the committee, in 1996, the scholarship was named in his memory.

Skaters who apply must be U.S. citizens and members of a Minnesota figure skating club. They are expected to have trained in Minnesota for at least nine months and to have passed the Intermediate free skating singles or pairs tests, or the bronze ice dance tests.

From 1993 through 1999, the scholarship fund derived support from the Minnesota *Ice Symphonies*. These festive events were headlined by nationally known skaters with a cast of Minnesota State Champion skaters. The first *Ice Symphony* was held in December 1993 at Mariucci Arena on the University of Minnesota campus. The Greater Twin Cities Youth Symphony provided the music and the star was national and world champion Todd Eldredge. He returned in 1995 for a second engagement. Michelle Kwan was the headliner of the *Ice Symphony* in 1996. Dorothy Hamill came in 1997 and Rudy Galindo was the star for the following year. The last *Ice Symphony* was held in 1999 at the Parade Ice Garden and the stars were national champion ice dancers Elizabeth Punsalan and Jerod Swallow.

The Long Blade Skaters

Not all clubs exist to teach, test, and perform. Having a time and place to skate is enough for the long bladers, whose club dates to about 1950. Their recreational skating sessions are held in the mornings at Aldrich arena, or the Breck, Blaine, or Augsburg rinks, depending on the season and availability of ice time. In earlier times long blade skaters could be seen at the Hippodrome, the Minneapolis Arena, or the Ice Center. The long blade group at the Arena once numbered over two hundred skaters who took to the ice on Sunday mornings, and Tuesday and Friday nights. All were accomplished skaters; Marion Curry recalled, "You could hear the swish, swish of their skates." At the Arena they skated to music played on a giant Wurlitzer pipe organ. The organist placed numbers indicating the pairs of songs he planned to play next. The number seven meant a tango and eight was a waltz. If someone fell, the observant organist would play crashing notes. Many members of today's club have been speed skaters or figure skaters. They made the switch because they enjoy the balance and long strokes of the long blade skates. The skates themselves are now difficult to locate, as one long blader said, "You watch for estate sales."

In Duluth a recreational skating club is the Monday morning group that has met since 1936. According to Ginny Johnson, they meet to skate, lunch, and then sometimes skate again.

Minnesota Ice Rinks

Forty-seven Minnesota figure skating clubs are affiliated with the USFS of which three are high school or college clubs and twenty belong to the TCFSA. Several clubs list ice availability at more than one rink, notably the Duluth FSC, Maplewood FSC, the Starlight Ice Dance Club (in Minneapolis), and the Plymouth Panda's FSC. The largest and newest facility is the Schwan Super Rink in the National Sports Center in Blaine which is the headquarters as well for the Northern Blades NSC FSC (organized as the White Bear FSC in 1998).

Minnesota's first indoor ice rinks were all built within its larger cities, often in the downtown areas. Skaters could often walk, take a streetcar, or ride a bus to these arenas. After World War II people began moving to the first ring suburban communities of the Twin Cities. Beginning in the 1950s schools, colleges and universities built rinks, mainly for hockey. Professional ice sports, high school tournaments, and touring ice shows were regular users of the Civic Center in St. Paul, the Met Sports Center in Bloomington, and the Target Center in Minneapolis. By the 1970s counties constructed recreational facilities for their burgeoning populations, but access was car-dependent so the new arenas sit in the midst of acres of parking.

Taking a look at the state of skating in Minnesota at the time of the 1973 U.S. Nationals, one writer noted that the Twin Cities then had 2 professional hockey teams (both have since left), 35 ice rinks with 28 of them built within the previous 5½ years, and sports associations that had held 3 outdoor speed skating championships (on Lakes Como, Minnetonka, and Nokomis) as well as the World Cup hockey matches, all in that one year. But using those 35 rinks were only 5 figure skating clubs. The rinks built included the $23 million St. Paul Civic Center and the $6 million Metropolitan Sports Center (both now razed) at the top end of the scale and the St. Mary's Point arena on the St. Croix River, built for $190,000, at the low end of the scale. In between were public arenas built in both Ramsey and Hennepin counties and private school arenas for Blake, Breck, and St. Paul Academy.[24]

For the amateur figure skater and the sports teams, another building boom offered new rinks, beginning in the 1990s. The construction program was called the Mighty Ducks legislation, after the trilogy of Disney films about a David and Goliath contest in the hockey world. Boys and men had always played hockey in Minnesota, but suddenly girls discovered the sport. The already-crowded schedules at many rinks became quite impossible. The solution was to build or expand rinks throughout the state.

First came a task force charged with discovering which Minnesota communities needed indoor ice facilities. Girls' ice hockey had already been sanctioned by the Minnesota State High School League in 1994 with the first girls' state hockey tournament (in the country) played in 1995. The task force found that nearly 90 communities needed indoor rinks.

Senator Jim Metzen and former Representative Bob Milbert guided successful legislation appropriating funds annually for either new arenas or the renovation of existing centers. The Minnesota Amateur Sports Commission was given the authority to allocate up to $100,000 for a renovation grant or up to $250,000 for a new ice center. Seventy-nine grants for new arenas were awarded through the Mighty Ducks Ice Arena Program (resulting in 61 new sheets of ice) and 74 grants were made to renovate existing facilities. The total investment made by the state was $18,405,000 from 1995-2004.

The Mighty Ducks program did not fund two very large skating venues. One is the John Rose Oval opened in 1993 in Roseville. The Oval is said to be the world's largest outdoor refrigerated ice sheet. It is used by the Roseville FSC and the Long Blade skaters as well as by the speed skaters.

The prize for the largest indoor skating venue will probably be held for many years to come by the Schwan Super Rink at the National Sports Center in Blaine. The 8 ice sheets join a soccer stadium, 52 soccer fields, an 18-hole golf course and now a dry land training facility for hockey.

The first phase of the Schwan Super Rink opened in 1998 with four Olympic-size rinks. On April 13, 2007, two Minnesota governors, Tim Pawlenty and Wendell Anderson, both former hockey players, helped dedicate the expanded Super Rink and the Herb Brooks Training Center

Support for the Super Rink addition came from the sale of the old Columbia Arena and from the cities of Blaine, Circle Pines, Centerville, and Lino Lakes. Anchor Bank lent $600,000 to Anoka County to cover construction costs with the expectation that rental fees would repay the loan. Hockey teams from Blaine, Centennial, Forest Lake, Tri-City, and Bethel University committed to using the rink as their headquarters as did the Herb Brooks Foundation.

While the four new rinks offer NHL-size ice, the restaurant is the Hat Trick Café, and there will be a display of Herb Brooks memorabilia in the Legacy Walk, the members of the Northern Blades FSC will not be ignored. They have the use of the ice, training rooms, and a coaching staff.

Given its size, the Schwan Super Rink would seem a very appropriate venue for competitions. That has already been the case with the ISI 2007 Synchronized Championships held just after the opening of the addition.

The USFS and ISI programs help a beginner learn to skate and then progress through test levels: the USFS' eight and the ISI's ten. The USFS program stresses competition while the ISI aids the recreational skater. The USFS is the U.S. governing body for the International Skating Union. Skaters qualify through its program for national, world, and Olympic competition. The ISI skater who has passed the appropriate test, said Jane Schaber of the National Skating School at Blaine, can enter national or world ISI events. There are no sectional or regional elimination competitions leading up to these championships. Skating clubs that sponsor synchro teams often belong to both the ISI and USFS. The FSC of Minneapolis, the Braemar-City of Lakes FSC, Woodbury FSC, the Roseville FSC, the Eagan Ice Crystal FSC, and the Northern Blades NSC FSC hold such dual affiliations.

❄ ❄ ❄ ❄ ❄ ❄ ❄ ❄

1. George Bryant. "That's How It Was, 1901-3," (1969). George Bryant Papers, P1704, Minnesota Historical Society.
2. Biloine Whiting Young and David Lanegran. *Grand Avenue: The Renaissance of an Urban Street*. St. Cloud, MN: North Star Press of St. Cloud Inc. (1996), 27-28.
3. Benjamin T. Wright. *op. cit.*, 17, 18.
4. *St. Paul Pioneer Press*, June 30, 1940.
5. Others state that the idea should be credited to Orrin Markhus, the club's pro.
6. *St. Paul Dispatch*, July 18, 1945, 17.
7. Norman Katkov. "Embattled Twins," *Holiday*, February 1951, 35. The photograph is by George Leavens.
8. John H. Harvey. "Summer Ice Festival as polished as ever," *St. Paul Pioneer Press*, July 15, 1977.
9. John H. Harvey. *St. Paul Pioneer Press*, undated clipping.
10. Gareth Hiebert. "Show of the People," *Saint Paul is My Beat*. St. Paul: North Central Publishing Company (1958), 138-139.
11. Kevin Driscoll. "Coming Full Circle. Skating Club figures on a Pleasant return to St. Paul," *Highland Villager*, January 14, 2004, 38.
12. *St. Paul Pioneer Press*, August 23, 1943, 13.
13. Greg Kirschling. "Memories on Ice," *Duluth News-Tribune*, June 28, 1998, E1,9.
14. "Varied Program Marks Auditorium Celebration," *Rochester Post-Bulletin*, undated clipping.
15. Andrea Faiad. "She'll be the judge of that," *Rochester Post-Bulletin*, February 19, 2000, 80.
16. Benjamin Wright called Thacker virtually unknown today, but along with Joan Tozzer one "of the finest exponents of compulsory figures…" Wright, *ibid*, 69.
17. *Rochester Post-Bulletin*, August 19, 1963, 14.
18. *Rochester Post-Bulletin*, May 24, 1972, 50.
19. Information from the Archives, University of Minnesota.
20. *1951 Gopher*, edited by Larry Pray. Minneapolis: Board in Control of Student Publications (1951), 180.
21. Gerri Walbert. "Alice Sue Claeys Has the World at Her Feet," *Skating*, July 1990, 21-22.
22. The TCFSA member clubs are the FSC of Bloomington, Braemar-City of Lakes FSC, Brooklyn Park FSC, Burnsville-Minnesota Valley FSC, Eden Prairie FSC, Lake Minnetonka FSC, Mankato FSC, Maplewood FSC, Chaska FSC, Eagan Ice Crystal FSC, Elk River FSC, Northern Blades FSC, FSC of Minneapolis, Rochester FSC, Roseville FSC, St. Cloud FSC, St. Paul FSC, Tri-County FSC, Woodbury FSC, and Starlight Ice Dance Club in Minneapolis.
23. *Rink Link*, March 1999, 4.
24. *1973 U.S. Nationals* program, 49.

Chapter Four

The Thrill of a Crowd: Skating in Shows

It all began on Sunday afternoons on St. Paul's Lake Como. Two young men came there to skate, but their style was somewhat different. Instead of concentrating on endless loops and turns, they did tricks, amazing and amusing anyone who happened by. They felt, as one later wrote, that figure skating could be fun and entertaining.[1] For many many years they proved that it could be. Those who saw Eddie Shipstad and Oscar Johnson's antics invited them to skate indoors at the Hippodrome. By the early 1920s, they were appearing in the Hippodrome club's carnivals, but probably their first big show was in 1925 at the new Minneapolis Arena.

In June of 1925, five thousand members of Kiwanis held their international convention in St. Paul. One huge parade of bands and Kiwanians marched from the state capitol to Rice Park. Dances filled the hotel ballrooms in the evenings and every inch of the St. Paul Auditorium was scheduled for all day meetings. People in St. Paul were asked to volunteer their cars to transport visitors from the depot to their hotels and to cut flowers from their gardens in case local florists ran out of blossoms for the delegates' wives. St. Paul officials wanted to make sure that everyone who attended the big convention would have a good time. The local organizers were sure that one evening's entertainment would be completely new to most of the visitors: a Midsummer Ice Carnival planned for the Minneapolis Arena.

On Wednesday, June 25th, a sold-out Arena crowd (the straw-hatted men were advised to wear jackets as the inside temperature would be in the rather frosty sixties) watched the festivities. First the American Legion Post #8 drum and bugle corps marched down the ice. Then a group of Blackfoot Indians from Glacier National Park came to "adopt" some of the visitors into their tribe and then give them a ride in a dogsled. The program continued with fancy skating by Ann Munkholm, Dr. Joe Goswitz and Lillian Goswitz. And there were exhibitions of trick or comic skating by Orrin Markhus,

Heinie Brock, Everett McGowan (who jumped over barrels), and John Davidson (who used stilt skates, an act he may have invented). Eddie Shipstad and Oscar Johnson were billed as a "comic and acrobatic act." The Kiwanians felt that it had been such a fine show that it should be repeated for the general public, so two encore performances took place.[2]

In 1927 Eddie Shipstad and Oscar Johnson were hired to perform during the intermissions of New York Rangers hockey games. They brought their Bowery routine and Spark Plug the Horse act to many new audiences.[3]

When they returned to Minnesota, their first effort was a carnival in Minneapolis called the *Greater Arena Ice Show*. It opened on the same day that the Bank Holiday was declared, so many tickets were paid for on credit or by barter. Their next two carnivals, produced for the Children's Hospital Association in St. Paul, were triumphs. In each case the casts included professional skaters with whom they had worked before and would later tour: Evelyn Chandler, Orrin Markhus, Heinie Brock, and, by now, Eddie's brother Roy, who had been the pro at the Duluth FSC. The programs featured many children of the CHA members and amateur skaters from the St. Paul and Minneapolis clubs like Dorothy Snell and Robin Lee.

There were four more carnivals or *Follies* produced for the Children's Hospital Association by the fledgling St. Paul FSC. The 1936 show was directed by Orrin Markhus. It was an elaborate production with a northern theme. A snow queen entered in a sled pulled by huskies. The following year the theme was nautical and the star was Evelyn Chandler whose "breath-taking spins, leaps, and abrupt stops" thrilled the crowd. All of the skating and comedy numbers dealt with events on shipboard or at the ports of call; even the ice was painted to show an ocean with North America at one end and South America at the other.[4] Miss Chandler returned to star in the 1938 show, but the next year (1939) was produced and directed by Maribel Vinson. One quite small member of the 1937 cast was a last minute addition. John Davidson, the stilt skater, had expected to perform but became ill. One of Markhus' youngest students, six-year-old Irene Davidson, was asked to take his place. She was a hit and just what Hollywood wanted. Renamed "Irene Dare," she starred in several musical comedies as a skater. Of her first film, *Breaking the Ice* (1938), a *New York Times* reporter wrote, "Little Miss Dare is neither Sonja Henie or Shirley Temple. She is just a cute youngster of six who knows how to skate."[5]

Her co-stars were Charles Ruggles, Dolores Costello, Lew Ayres, and Bobby Breen. One advertisement for the RKO Radio picture said, "The boy with the golden voice and the girl with the silver skates bring happiness and laughter." Dare's second movie, *Everything's On Ice* (1939), was set in

Florida, on an ice rink. In her last known film, *Silver Skates* (1942), Irene Dare worked with Frick and Frack. Her short career shows that Hollywood was interested in skating films and producers liked the novelty of a very young actress.[6]

Large Touring Ice Shows

Years later Bob Murphy, a local newspaper columnist, interviewed Lyle Wright, the manager of the Minneapolis Arena. Wright told Murphy of trying to export the Shipstads and Johnson show to northern Minnesota. Duluth didn't welcome the show, Wright said, because they preferred amateur skaters. Eveleth didn't warm to the show either. In fact, Eveleth was so cold that horn players didn't dare put mouths to instruments for fear of becoming stuck, so the music that night on the Range was played by the violins.[7]

Then in early 1935 they were asked by Edward Mahlke, a Chicago newspaperman, to put together a show for the Hotel Sherman in Chicago. The show at the hotel's College Inn was to be a short, perhaps one-month-long engagement, but the run eventually lasted sixteen months. Mahlke, who died in 1938, briefly became a partner of the Shipstads and Johnson in their next venture, the *Ice Follies*. In later years the *Ice Follies* did appear

Postcard view of the College Inn's ice rink at the Hotel Sherman in Chicago. Eddie Shipstad and Oscar Johnson skated here in their first long-running show.

The staff and cast of the Ice Follies *leave St. Paul for Tulsa on their first road trip, November 1936.*

regularly in Duluth, always publicizing their skaters with local connections like Roy Shipstad, Bess Ehrhardt, and the Maxsons.

Jill Shipstad Thomas, Roy Shipstad's daughter, told an interviewer that the concept of the show and the name, *Ice Follies*, both came from Duluth. Roy and Eddie Shipstad and Oscar Johnson had appeared in a show for the Duluth FSC in 1924. They were inspired by that experience, she said, when they developed their own show for Children's Hospital in St. Paul and then called their touring production *Ice Follies* as well.[8]

In November 1936 the show, by now known as Shipstads and Johnson's *Ice Follies*, loaded its cast and all their baggage onto a bus and headed for Oklahoma. First stop: Tulsa. It took a while to build interest and audiences for something so new. And there were problems. Tulsa was under quarantine because of a polio epidemic. At the next stop, Kansas City, there was a heavy snowstorm, but gradually the crowds grew so that there were more people in the seats than on the ice. In the 1946 program, attendance was said to be approaching three million people per year.

The driver of the Greyhound bus on that first tour was Bertrum "Bert" Lundblad, who became the company's executive vice president and general manager. His wife, Isabel (known as "Bisa" or Busy Isabel) was *Follies* wardrobe director for over 40 years. One friend commented that the show could not have gone on without her. She "knew how to make costumes that would last through 400-plus performances."[9]

From a few stops in the early years, the *Ice Follies* schedule grew to a forty-six-week tour by 1941. In many cities the show spent a week or more. By its 10th anniversary in 1946, the city of Minneapolis took notice of its

Roy and Eddie Shipstad and Oscar Johnson, the founders of the Ice Follies.

success and expressed its appreciation. Every year, in normal times, the Follies brought between 57,000 and 60,000 people into Minneapolis to see its shows. They came by bus and train from small towns all over Minnesota and neighboring states. In fact 40 percent of those "free-spending" people came from out-of-town. *Ice Follies* performances at the Arena consistently sold out, wrote Charles Johnson in his sports column. People often waited

Eddie Shipstad (the nanny) and Oscar Johnson (the cop) developed many comic routines for their Ice Follies programs.

around before a performance, hoping that someone would have unwanted tickets to sell.[10] The Civic and Commerce Association held a luncheon on April 4, 1946, at the Radisson Hotel to show its thanks to the Shipstads and Oscar Johnson. Governor Edward Thye and Mayor Hubert H. Humphrey headed the list of civic leaders honoring the ice show founders for creating such a successful business.[11]

Brenda Ueland saw the show in 1946 and noted how she thought it had improved since she'd last seen it. She liked the skating, the costumes, and the music, but she found one aspect of the performance significant: everyone seemed to like what they were doing. She wrote in her column, "Those kids, skating and flying, going backwards 60 miles an hour on one silver point, can't keep from smiling with wild frolicksomeness. It is as though everybody was continually shouting 'Whee!'"[12]

Even after the headquarters of the *Ice Follies* organization was moved to California, programs pointed to the show's Minnesota connections. Among the featured skaters were Ruby and Bobby Maxson, and Lois Dworshak from Duluth, Betty Schalow from St. Paul, and the various twins from the Twin Cities. From Minneapolis were the Scotvolds (Joyce and Joanne) and the

Joyce and Joanne Scotvold, Follies stars from 1947-54, autographed this photograph for their friend, Janet Gerhauser Carpenter.

Mary and Jane Thomas were performing poodles in the "Crazy Quilt Circus" number of the Ice Follies *1944 season.*

Pastors (Jean and Joan). From St. Paul were Joanne and Sally Keogh, and the Thomases (Mary and Jane). While in later years auditions were announced whenever the *Ice Follies* came to Minnesota, several former *Follies* members recall being discovered at the Arena. Most were in high school when they were hired but had skated and often competed for years before turning pro. Jean Pastor said that when she and her twin were discovered, Eddie Shipstad saw them skating at the Arena and offered them a contract. They replied that they would have to ask their parents who felt that their minister should also be consulted. Reverend Reuben K. Youngdahl of Mount Olivet Lutheran Church told them to go ahead since "when opportunity knocks, it seldom knocks twice." While Pastor was a member of the *Ice Follies*, it felt like a family to her. She considered it the most wonderful opportunity she ever had.

The happiness of the skaters was genuine, according to Marion Curry. For her being a Folliette was a golden moment.[13] Like the Pastor twins, she'd been discovered at the Arena. Her first salary was $55 per week with a raise of $5 after the first six weeks. After signing their contracts, skaters reported to San Francisco where the show rehearsed at the Winterland

Arena, skating last year's numbers at night and the new ones during the day. Each year Folliettes learned five numbers in which they had assigned positions and then two more, to spare.

At the show skaters each had a spot in the dressing room where their costumes hung behind their chairs. Often their big hats were kept in special containers backstage while some of the huge heavy skirts were placed near the ice so a skater could just pull the costume on when needed. Between numbers the Folliettes sat around in bathrobes backstage and, if there was time, knitted. Argyle socks were popular at the time.

There were rules to follow and fines if the rules were broken. Folliettes were expected to be on time, not become overweight or have dirty skates. In Montreal they were warned not to go skiing for fear of an accident. There were weekly weigh-ins conducted by Mary Jane Lewis, the ballet mistress. Ms. Lewis led a mandatory weekly ballet class. Marion Curry recalled her ability to do arabesques "to the sky." Fran Claudet, who was a former Canadian junior champion, taught the skating class.

Since the *Follies* spent several days or more in most tour cities, there was time to see the sights—the museums, famous homes, stores, or the Hershey chocolate factory. Every night backstage there would be boxes of camellias or gardenias for the skaters. There were other special moments. Marion Curry can still remember the goose bumps she felt in San Francisco when VJ Day was proclaimed and the band captured the feeling by playing "Happy Days Are Here Again."

Marion Rudie Curry is the tenth Folliette in this line of precision skaters in the Ice Follies *of 1948.*

Heinie Brock lettered in baseball and swimming at the University of Minnesota before finding a home as a comic skater with the Shipstads and Johnson.

Opening Night at the Pan-Pacific Auditorium in Los Angeles was the beginning of every new year of touring. Not only was it exciting to see all the elements they had rehearsed come together, but there was another thrill. All the stars came. The glittering personalities of the movie world were in the audience. Mr. and Mrs. Ronald Reagan always attended. So did Bob Hope and

Right: Phyllis and Harris Legg (wearing stilt skates) and Bobby and Ruby Maxson were in "Be Young Again" from the Ice Follies of 1942.

Below: Bobby and Ruby Maxson, a brother-sister pair from Duluth, joined the Ice Follies *after high school.*

Cesar Romero. Another Folliette remembered the shock of taking her bow and realizing that, right then, right there, Clark Gable was looking straight at her.

Certain acts became famous and expected parts of *Ice Follies* shows: Heinie Brock and his barrel jumping, Phyllis and Harris Legg who skated on stilts, the cantilevered Swiss pair Frick and Frack doing their spread eagles,

Left: Betty Schalow, shown skidding to a stop, skated in the St. Paul Pop Concerts before beginning her long career with the Ice Follies as a soloist.

Below: Roy Shipstad as Mr. Debonair, accompanied by Janet Raymond and Ginger Morrison.

A perennial favorite of audiences was the "The Swing Waltz", here shown in the version from the Ice Follies *of 1940.*

Evelyn Chandler's butterfly jump, Harris Legg's soaring leap through a flaming hoop, Roy Shipstad as the elegant "Mr. Debonair," and the formally dressed couples who danced "The Swing Waltz." The leads in "The Swing Waltz" were first skated by Roy Shipstad and Lois Dworshak. In 1941 a new brother-sister pair, the Maxsons, was assigned to skate the number. They did it so well that, according to Oscar Johnson, "If we had to cut the *Ice Follies* to just one number, it would be the Swing Waltz we would retain. Audiences everywhere never seem to tire of it. And Bobby and Ruby are ideal as the anchor pair."[14]

Shipstads and Johnson's *Ice Follies* was the first of the major figure skating shows to tour nationally. The *Follies* appeared mainly in northern and eastern cities which had rinks with adequate seating capacity. In New York City the *Follies* appeared at Madison Square Garden before an opening night crowd of 10,000. Maribel Y. Vinson reviewed the show for *The New York Times* calling it a "brilliant revue on skates" and acrobatic rather than artistic.

CREATORS AND ORIGINATORS OF THE WORLD'S FIRST ICE EXTRAVAGANZA

SHIPSTADS
& JOHNSON

18TH ANNUAL EDITION

Ice Follies

of 1954

OFFICIAL PUBLICATION

A beautiful girl in an elegant costume (short skirt, long gloves)was the usual design for an Ice Follies *program cover. Several* Ice Capades *covers were designed by pin-up master George Petty.*

She gave high praise to Heinie Brock's barrel act and Dying Duck and the skating of Roy Shipstad, who kept "spinning as if he'd never stop."[15]

Competition for the *Follies* came all too soon. Sonja Henie's first professional tour began in the spring of 1936 but went to only a few cities. Her plan was to spend part of every year making movies and the rest of the time touring with her show, *Hollywood on Ice*, which has managed by Arthur Wirtz of Chicago. The first tour began in March and by April included Minneapolis.

There was an almost immediate problem. On the eve of her opening at the Arena, the USFSA refused a request to allow amateur skaters in her program. So the Henie show became a totally professional exhibition featuring Norval Baptie and Gladys Lamb, Orrin Markhus, Margaret Bennett, McGowan and Mack, Heinie Brock, and Maud the Skating Mule (with Eddie Shipstad and Oscar Johnson inside). Jack Dunn, the English star, was her partner for the three-day-performance. Ms. Henie was proud to note that her show's opening night had attracted two hundred more patrons than had been present at Evelyn Chandler's pro-amateur ice show a short time earlier.[16]

The *Ice Capades*, *Holiday on Ice*, the *Ice Vanities*, the *Ice Cycles* and the *All-European Ice Revue* were the next rivals on the entertainment calendar, many of which had Minnesota connections. Ice show founders have been either skaters like the Shipstads and Johnson, Sonja Henie or Tom Collins, or business leaders. Arena owners founded the *Ice Capades* as a touring show that would appear in the venues they controlled. John H. Harris of Pittsburgh was the founding president and continued in the post for many years. The *Ice Capades* opened in February 1941 at the arena in Hershey, Pennsylvania. One early program carried the somewhat apologetic admission that while they realized that the war had begun, the promoters still felt the country deserved entertainment.

As one Minneapolis columnist reported, the *Ice Capades* mixed patriotism with skating as the war continued. In one of his columns Cedric Adams wrote first of the show's need for skaters. The *Ice Capades* was appearing in St. Paul in February and wanted to find at least a dozen girl skaters who could expect to earn at least $55 per week. There were rules to follow, he wrote, and the pay would be docked if the skaters were late for rehearsal, did not care for their costumes, or smoked. Then he mentioned the current show, set in the south Pacific:

My Dear Friend: *Del Conroy*

I have your Audition Card for "ICE-CAPADES" and I wish your attention to the following memo on same . . .

Could develop Into be good Skater

Would you be so good as to advise me your reaction as to sa so that I might indicate on our records. We do thank you for Auditioning with us and we are continua looking for Talent. We want to know your interest.

Most sincerely yours,

JOHN H. HARRIS, President
ICE-CAPADES, INC.

Please address your reply to John H. Harris, Ice-Capades, Wm. Penn Hotel, Pittsburgh, Pa.

Del Conroy auditioned for the Ice Capades, but joined the U.S.Army Air Corps instead. He later skated in hundreds of Pop Concerts and programs of the St. Paul FSC.

SHIPSTADS & JOHNSON *Itinerary* ICE FOLLIES 1956

SCHEDULE

LOS ANGELES	SEPT. 8 - OCT. 2, 1955	Pan Pacific, 7600 Beverly Blvd.
DENVER	OCT. 4 - OCT. 9	Denver Coliseum, East 46th and Humboldt
DES MOINES	OCT. 11 - OCT. 16	Veterans Memorial Auditorium
CHICAGO	OCT. 18 - OCT. 30	The Chicago Stadium
CINCINNATI	NOV. 2 - NOV. 20	Cincinnati Gardens, 2250 Seymour Ave.
HERSHEY	NOV. 23 - DEC. 3	Sports Arena
NEW HAVEN	DEC. 4 - DEC. 11	The Arena, Grove Street at Orange
CHRISTMAS VACATION	DEC. 12 - DEC. 24	Christmas Vacation
PHILADELPHIA	DEC. 25, '55 - JAN. 15, '56	The Arena, 45th and Market Sts.
CLEVELAND	JAN. 17 - JAN. 29	The Arena, 3700 Euclid Avenue
TORONTO	JAN. 30 - FEB. 3	Maple Leaf Gardens, 60 Carlton
MONTREAL	FEB. 5 - FEB. 12	The Forum, 2313 St. Catherine St., West
BOSTON	FEB. 14 - FEB. 26	Boston Gardens, North Station
PROVIDENCE	FEB. 27 - MARCH 4	Rhode Island Auditorium, 1111 No. Main St.
BUFFALO	MARCH 6 - MARCH 11	Memorial Auditorium
SYRACUSE	MARCH 13 - MARCH 18	Onondaga County War Memorial
PITTSBURGH	MARCH 20 - MARCH 27	The Gardens, 110 N. Craig St.
MINNEAPOLIS	MARCH 29 - APRIL 15	The Arena, 2900 Dupont Avenue So.
MILWAUKEE	APRIL 18 - APRIL 22	The Arena, 410 West Kilbourn Ave.
WINNIPEG	APRIL 24 - APRIL 28	Winnipeg Arena, 333 Main St.
SPOKANE	MAY 1 - MAY 7	Spokane Coliseum
SEATTLE	MAY 9 - MAY 20	Civic Ice Arena, 4th North and Mercer Sts.
ANNUAL VACATION	MAY 21 - JUNE 20	Annual Vacation
SAN FRANCISCO	JUNE 21 - SEPT. 2	Winterland, Post and Steiner Streets

TELL YOUR FRIENDS AND RELATIVES THE ICE FOLLIES SPECIAL IS HEADED THEIR WAY—

Remind them of our playing dates in their home towns so they, too, may enjoy a wonderful evening of entertainment at the ICE FOLLIES.

ICE FOLLIES SPECIAL

By 1955-56 the Ice Follies traveled in its own train to the mainly northern cities on its schedule. Drawings here include a Folliette and a skating lantern that one of her ancestors might have carried while skating on a Minnesota lake in the evening.

> Sixty-four girls skate out on the ice, each carrying a
> replica of a B-25 plane. The girls assemble the bomber
> in $2^{1}/_{2}$ minutes flat on the ice. The finale has a take off
> effect that is amazing.[17]

Robin Lee, skating with Donna Atwood as his partner, was an early *Ice Capades* star. When he left for military service, his replacement was Bobby Specht who in turn was followed by Jimmy Lawrence. Specht returned to spend many years with the *Capades*. Other *Ice Capades* stars from the Upper Midwest included Lois Dworshak, Orrin Markhus and Irma Thomas, continuing their "Old Smoothies" act, and Patti Phillippi who had been a baton twirling champion (with the Hamm's Brewery marching band, the "Indians") and used her ability as a twirler once she became a skater.

An indication of the popularity of the touring ice shows is shown in the itineraries published in the program for the Olympic Figure Skating Tryouts in Chicago in December 1947.[18] That year the *Ice Follies* made appearances in twenty cities beginning in Los Angeles in September and ending in San Francisco in June. Their stay in Minneapolis lasted from April 16-May 9, 1948, at the Minneapolis Arena. The *Ice Capades* opened in Pittsburgh in September and closed in Los Angeles in June. Their Minnesota stop was from February 25-March 2, 1948, at the St. Paul Auditorium. *Holiday on Ice* played in Mexico and Canada but not in Minnesota. Their thirty-three stops began in White Plains, New York, and ended in Salt Lake City. Sonja Henie's company was not listed, but a smaller troupe, the *Ice Cycles*, was. They opened in Dallas and finished the run of twenty-four cities in San Diego. *Ice Cycles* appeared at the Mayo Civic Auditorium in Rochester from April 1-6, 1948. Not only were there now a number of skating companies, but there were job opportunities in the theatrical skating field.

The *Ice Cycles* did not last long as an independent show, but it did have a Minnesota connection. Minneapolis skater Marjorie Lang and her sister Kay joined the *Ice Follies* in 1939. After a few years Marjorie Lang was asked to become skating director of the *Ice Cycles*. Her husband, Chris Kelley, served as road manager. Material about Mrs. Kelley's career is in the collections of the Hennepin History Museum. Other companies that appeared in Minnesota cities during the 1930s and 1940s were the *Ice Vanities* and the *All-European Ice Revue*. In 1940 the Hibbing Jaycees sponsored a visit by the *Ice Vanities* to the Hibbing Memorial Arena. Another stop on that tour was Duluth. The star of the show was Vivi-Anne Hultén. The *All-European Ice Revue* appeared at the Minneapolis Arena with Edwina Blades and an American, Audrey Peppe.

HOLIDAY ON ICE

SOUVENIR PROGRAM · TWENTY-FIVE CENTS

Holiday on Ice *program for the 1947 season.*

Both the *Ice Follies* and the *Ice Capades* had companies headed by female stars (Evelyn Chandler for the Follies and Donna Atwood for the Capades) and chorus lines (the Folliettes and Ice Capets). Both companies based their itineraries on cities with existing ice arenas. *Holiday on Ice*, which began in 1943, chose another method. They brought the ice to the city, which allowed the show to travel almost anywhere. The company carried portable rinks; while one was in use, the other was sent ahead to the next stop. In the 1940s *Holiday on Ice* appeared in Mexico. With the portable rinks, even Africa could be scheduled, and was. Roy Blakey, who skated in the show's European tour as well as in Asia, remembers the thrill of skating on a rink set in Malaga's bullring with a view of mountains in the distance. Stops on these foreign tours were often as long as a month and very lucrative as skating shows were such a novelty in these cities at the time.

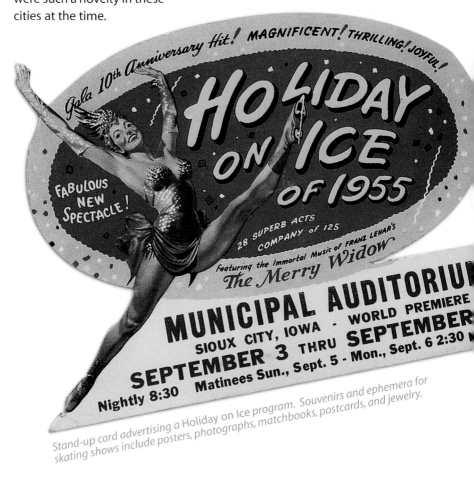

Stand-up card advertising a Holiday on Ice program. Souvenirs and ephemera for skating shows include posters, photographs, matchbooks, postcards, and jewelry.

Morris Chalfen during a trip to Moscow, 1963.

Holiday on Ice opened in Toledo in December 1943. The founders chose the name because of its Christmastime starting date. The Gilbert brothers and Minneapolis businessman Morris Chalfen (1907-1979) took over the company two years later. There were tours of South America in 1949, Europe in 1950, Japan in 1959, and Africa in 1960. Negotiations with the Russian Ministry of Culture to allow a Holiday on Ice appearance in Moscow led to a reciprocal arrangement. Holiday on Ice could play in the Russian capital if the company's promoter would bring the Moscow Circus and the Moiseyev dancers to America. The Holiday on Ice company was sold to Frank "Skee" Goodhart in 1973. Skee and his skating partner Lea (Ed Leary) were from Minneapolis and had done trick skating for the Ice Follies in the manner of Frick and Frack. But before that sale, Morris Chalfen had made a heroic "save."

Sonja Henie had broken with Arthur Wirtz, the longtime producer of her traveling show. She wanted to produce her own tour without his assistance. He continued to produce the *Hollywood Ice Revue*, but with Barbara Ann Scott in the lead role Sonja Henie had once had. When she tried to manage her own tour in 1952, she discovered that it was a very difficult task when at least three other skating shows were competing for arenas. Chalfen persuaded Sonja Henie to headline his European company and even make an appearance in Oslo, where she had not been since before World War II. It was a triumph. Ms. Henie ended her twenty years of touring with skating shows in 1956 as the star of the European company of *Holiday on Ice*.[19]

One man who had skated with both Sonja Henie's *Hollywood Ice Revue* and *Holiday on Ice* became the tour manager for the latter and eventually helped create a very successful new ice show. Tom Collins, born in Kirkland Lake, Ontario, joined *Holiday on Ice* in 1949 as a chorus skater. He moved into a role as a pairs skater, and by the early 1960s he was the star of the show. His sister Marty joined the cast and married the owner, Morris

Tom Collins, co-creator of Champions on Ice.

The cast of Champions on Ice 2006. Seated in front are Tatiana Totmyanina and Maxim Marinin. Second row: Surya Bonaly, Sasha Cohen, Michelle Kwan, Irina Slutskaya, Kimmie Meissner, Marina Anissina, and Irina Grigorian. Third row: Evgeni Plushenko, Vladimir Besedin, Gwendal Peisserat. Fourth row: Evan Lysacek, Viktor Petrenko, Rudy Galindo, Johnny Weir. Fifth row: Ben Agosto, Tanith Belbin, Oleksiy Polishchuk, Dan Hollander.

Chalfen. After her death in 1960, Collins felt he wanted to move to the management side of skating, and rose to the post of vice president of *Holiday on Ice*.[20] Tom Collins and Morris Chalfen launched the World Champions Figure Skating Exhibition in 1969 with tour stops in fifteen cities— eight in Canada and seven in the United States. It was based on the premise that after the World Championships took place, audiences would be interested in the new title holders. A show of exhibition skating by the newly-crowned single skaters, pairs, and ice dancers would offer a change and variety from the other shows with their ballets, elaborate costumes, and staging. It would be a show of skaters rather than a skating show. The skaters would appear with the sanction of the USFSA and would be, paid which, of course, was a revolutionary concept but one welcomed by the skaters.

At first the tour only took place once the World Championships, held every third year in North America, had ended. Beginning in 1983 the tour became an annual affair. The 1994 tour, after the Lillehammer Olympics and the Tonya Harding-Nancy Kerrigan affair, was one of the best attended.[21] As Tom Collins once remarked, "What those two girls did for skating was unbelievable!"

Although the tour's name has changed several times, the idea behind *Champions on Ice*, as it is called today, remains the same. It tours only in North America. Over the years its casts have included virtually every eligible national or world champion. Jill Trenary, as ladies' world title-holder in 1990, is the only Minnesotan to have toured with the show. Some skaters have continued to headline later shows, both the usual spring event and a winter tour that began in 1996.[22] Brian Boitano, Michelle Kwan, Dorothy Hamill, and Viktor Petrenko have all spent years performing with *Champions on Ice*.

Ever since the 1978 tour, Tom Collins has made a practice of inviting an up-and-coming local figure skater to perform. His invitation then went to Brian Boitano. In 2007 Alex Johnson from the Braemar-City of Lakes FSC and the 2007 U.S. novice silver medalist, skated with the show in Minneapolis. Rohene Ward, a national competitor from the FSC of Minneapolis, was invited to perform in 2006.

Management of the *Champions on Ice* tours continues to be in the hands of the Collins family. Tom Collins Enterprises Inc. included his brothers Butch and Harris, and now his three sons are on the staff. Harris Collins, creative director and choreographer, died during a *Champions on Ice* performance in Chicago in 1996. The Minnesota Skating Scholarship was named after him.

Champions on Ice was acquired by AEG (Anschutz Entertainment Group) in November 2006. AEG was named to manage Target Center in April 2007.

Both the Ice Capades and the Ice Follies went through several changes in ownership and the former eventually shut its doors for good. The Ice Follies was sold to the Shasta Corporation of Fresno, California, and then to the Medical Investment Corporation of Minneapolis (headed by Tom Scallen). Feld Entertainment, which already owned Ringling Brothers and Barnum and Bailey, acquired both Holiday on Ice and the Ice Follies. In 1980 the Felds worked out an arrangement with the Walt Disney Company to license Disney characters, music, and stories in the ice shows. Thus, Disney on Ice was born. The change from the Ice Follies shows of the past was complete. As one critic said, "The mouse ate skating." Disney on Ice shows could use tales and characters developed for Walt Disney films and musicals. Gig Siruno played Mowgli in a production of The Jungle Book. He is now the company's performance director. Kristina Olson is currently with the ice show, appearing in scenes from Pinocchio.

Ice Follies history lives on in another way. After they retired from the show, skaters often returned to Minnesota to enter college, take other jobs, and/or marry. Through an Ex-Folliettes organization, they keep in contact and celebrate occasions like the 50th anniversary of the Ice Follies in 1986. That year a special performance of Disney on Ice was held at the Met Sports Center. In a ceremony, a plaque was placed on the wall of the Rainbow grocery store that is located on part of the land where the Minneapolis Arena once stood.[23]

Oscar Johnson's memory is honored as well. As a child he had skated on the ponds near the Northern Pacific shops in St. Paul. In other seasons he and neighborhood kids used the area for different sports and games. On a visit to Minnesota at the time of an Ice Follies appearance in 1944, he met old friends for dinner and they decided to call themselves the Shop Pond Gang. The Gang raised money to support local teams in hockey, baseball, and speed skating who all wore distinctive green and white jackets. After Johnson's death in 1970, the skating arena at 1039 DeCourcy Circle near Energy Park Drive in St. Paul, was named in his memory.

Smaller Ice Shows

A show with a portable rink (smaller than those used by Holiday on Ice) and set up in a hotel (like Dorothy Lewis'), was Dorothy Franey's idea. She had won an Olympic medal in 1932 for speed skating, then turned to organizing skating shows by the 1940s. A story in the St. Paul paper announced that she had set up a company to offer skating shows on a small 40 by 60 foot rink that would be brought to the location. She would provide the equipment including a canvas tank and pipes to make ice within ten hours of set up. She planned to hire skaters who had worked with the Sonja Henie troupe. Her first destination was to be Mexico City followed by bookings in Denver and Dallas. Perhaps before that, according to an undated newspaper ad, Ms. Franey appeared in her *Star Spangled Revue* at the Terrace Café of the Hotel Lowry in St. Paul.

In Dallas her ice show was booked into the Century Room of the Hotel Adolphus for one month to present three shows per day. The engagement lasted fourteen years. The Century Room had a retractable wooden floor on which the rink could be placed. Although it was small, according to Miss Franey, you could do all the tricks. The article about Dorothy Franey's new venture concluded:

> The slender St. Paul girl who outraced the finest women
> skaters in the country just wasn't satisfied with being
> only a national champion. She is adding to the St. Paul
> tradition of ice show stars which was started by the
> Shipstad brothers, Oscar Johnson, and Dorothy Lewis.
> And the St. Paul Hippodrome was the skating
> springboard to fame for all of them.[24]

According to Dorothy Franey's son, Jimmy Langkop, his mother retired from the ice revue business around 1957. Until then she had booked three different troupes of skaters into entertainment venues. She planned the costumes, music, and choreography.[25]

Other Minnesota skaters took their acts or complete shows—finding other skaters—on the road, using portable ice rinks. The Leary brothers appeared at county fairs. McGowan and Mack headlined a traveling show. Dorothy Lewis, in addition to the permanent engagements at hotels, did some touring as well.

Minnesota Skaters and the Movies

A few Minnesota skaters have appeared in films, with Irene Dare perhaps being the first. Following the success of Sonja Henie's movies, other producers were eager to find stories and skaters for their projects. Dorothy Lewis was a featured actress in *Ice Capades of 1941*, also starring

Jerry Colonna and Phil Silvers. In Duluth, movie advertisements mentioned "Duluth's HomeTown Girls—Lois Dworshak, Carol Brown, and JoAnn Bartholdi." Lois Dworshak skated with the *Ice Follies*, the *Ice Vanities*, and the *Ice Capades*. She was known as the "jitterbug queen of the ice" for her rhythm swing dance. Others from the world of skating in the film were Belita, Phil Taylor and his daughter Megan. *The Ice Capades Revue* appeared the following year. In its cast were other skaters from the show, including Robin Lee.

Joan Crawford headlined *Ice Follies* (1939) with Jimmy Stewart as her co-star. Eddie and Roy Shipstad and Oscar Johnson appeared as themselves in that movie, but Bess Ehrhardt was given a new name for her part. When shown in Minnesota, advertisements mentioned the *Follies* stars, "and Duluth's own Ann Haroldson." Ms. Haroldson won the first Midwestern sectional senior ladies title in 1933. A photo caption noted that her coaches had been Roy Shipstad in Duluth and Charlotte in New York City.[26]

More recently *Ice Castles* (1978) was filmed in Minnesota with scenes set at various local rinks. Kelsey Ufford of the FSC of Minneapolis appeared in the film. Kirsten Olson was featured as "Nikki the Jumping Shrimp" in *Ice Princess* (2005).

❄ ❄ ❄ ❄ ❄ ❄ ❄ ❄

1. Oscar Johnson. "The History of the Ice Follies," *Ice Follies* program (1946).
2. *St. Paul Pioneer Press*, June 25, 1925, 1.
3. "St. Paulites' 'Spark Plug' Act Changed Skating Shows," *St. Paul Pioneer Press*, April 8, 1934, 3:4.
4. *St. Paul Pioneer Press*, April 3, 1937, 12.
5. *The New York Times*, September 23, 1938.
6. Rolf J. Canton. *Minnesotans in the Movies*, Minneapolis: Nodin Press (2007), 47-9.
7. Bob Murphy. "Reporting at Large," *Minneapolis Star*, January 24, 1962, 1C.
8. *Duluth New-Tribune*, February 15, 2002.
9. Ozzie St. George. "Follies' Isabel Lundblad Dies." *St. Paul Pioneer Press*, June 19, 1980, 25.
10. Charles Johnson. "Lowdown on Sports," *Minneapolis Star Journal*, April 4, 1946, 31.
11. *Minneapolis Daily Times*, March 28, 1946, 12.
12. Brenda Ueland. "What Goes on Here," *Minneapolis Daily Times*, March 25, 1946, 11.
13. Marion Curry. "Memories of a Golden Moment," Manuscript (2007).
14. Walter Kiley. "Swing Waltz No. 1 Act; Maxsons Put it over," *The New York Times*, undated clipping, circa 1941.
15. Maribel Y. Vinson. "Brilliant Acrobatic Skating Marks Professional Ice Carnival at the Garden," *The New York Times*, January 12, 1937, 12.
16. "Sonja Outdraws Chandler in Debut as Professional in Ice Show at Arena," *Minneapolis Tribune*, April 10, 1936, 28.
17. Cedric Adams. "In This Corner," *Minneapolis Star Journal*, February 14, 1944, 22.
18. *Olympic Figure Skating Tryouts* program, December 1947, 41-2.
19. James R. Hines. *Figure Skating: A History* (2006), 288-290
20. Christine Brennan. *Champions on Ice: Twenty-five years of the Worlds' finest figure skaters* (2002), 38-42.
21. Christine Brennan. *ibid.*, 112.

22. *Ibid*, 124.
23. James M. Tarbox. "Ice Follies good skates for 50 years," *St. Paul Pioneer Press and Dispatch*, March 16, 1986, 3E.
24. Perry Dotson. "Dot Franey Organizes New Skating Revue," *St. Paul Pioneer Press*, undated clipping.
25. Telephone interview with Jimmy Langkop, June 16, 2007.
26. Illustration, *Golfer and Sportsman*, January-February 1938, 29.

Chapter Five

Figure Skating and the St. Paul Winter Carnival

From its earliest years, the St. Paul Winter Carnival has emphasized the sport and art of figure skating. An ice rink or two have usually been set in front of a Carnival's palace of ice or snow. Skating club members vied to use those outdoor rinks in the 1880s. Fancy skaters have often been invited to demonstrate their skills on the rinks for Carnival-goers.

For Louis Hill's Outdoor Sports Carnival of 1916 Louis Moen of the Buckbee-Mears Company drew the emblematic Carnival Girl dressed in a bright red skating coat and carrying a huge red and white muff. In her matching red skates, she cheerfully skated across that year's millions of buttons, badges, menus, programs, and posters.

Although the St. Paul Winter Carnival halted its activities from 1918 until 1937, through the Great War and much of the Great Depression, many Minnesota communities held their own winter sports events, usually involving skating in demonstrations or as entertainment. Twin Cities skaters were often invited to headline winter ice shows such as ones held in Hibbing or Rochester.

A group of experienced skaters from the Hippodrome, who called themselves the "Bennett skaters," went to Rochester in 1924 for such a show. The municipal rink was outdoors at 7th Place S.E. just off 3rd Avenue. As the newspaper described the scene:

> Hundreds of persons gathered on the high bank
> outside the enclosed rink early in the afternoon and
> occupied that vantage point throughout the
> performance. They contributed generously to the
> collection which was taken up. Those who entered the
> rink paid a fee of twenty-five cents.[1]

Above: Members of the Minnehaha Skating Club gather for their Winter Carnival portrait, 1896.

Left: Margaret Bennett shown skating on Cedar Lake, 1923. She won the U.S. junior ladies' title and later became a coach for the FSC of Minneapolis.

Right: Ruth Larson Wadsworth, another Cedar Lake skater, was part of many Minneapolis skating programs.

Below: A crowd gathers to watch fancy skating on Lake Como during the St. Paul Winter Carnival of 1917.

Those who skated for the Rochester crowd included A. C. Bennett and his daughter Margaret, Ruth and Joe Gunberg, C. L. Christenson, Ruth Larson Wadsworth, and Julius Nelson who had once lived in Rochester. Oscar Johnson and Eddie Shipstad did cartwheels and handsprings. Then, wrote the impressed reporter, Eddie whirled on one foot in a squatting position.

For their Third Annual *Ice Follies* (December 28, 1937), the Hibbing Junior Chamber of Commerce invited another group of skaters, mostly from the St. Paul FSC, to perform. Skating as either solos or pairs were Margaret Grant, Janette Ahrens, Mary Louise Premer, the Thomas twins, and three members of the Preusch family.

During the 1930s, as mentioned earlier, the Shipstad brothers and Oscar Johnson organized ice skating shows at both the Minneapolis Arena and the St. Paul Auditorium annex. The audience for ice skating shows was growing. In 1937 business leaders in St. Paul decided to revive the Winter Carnival.

Each year Carnival organizers planned parades and rites such as the coronation of the queen and the storming of the ice palace by Vulcanus Rex the Fire King and his Krewe. Interspersed in the basic schedule came races, winter sports championships, and ice carnivals.

The following year (1938) the Ice Palace of 20,000 ice blocks was built in Mounds Park at Hastings Avenue and Mounds Boulevard, on the city's east side. It was an unusual design for the temporary abode of Boreas the Ice King, a semicircle without the towers or turrets of most of its predecessors. As a stage backdrop for performances on the rink in front, the design functioned well. The skating highlight of the Carnival was a five-day run of the *Gay Blades Revue* at the St. Paul Arena, starring Vivi-Anne Hultén, the Swedish star, and Karl Schaefer, the world and Austrian champion. Others in the cast of the touring show were Freddy Mesot of Belgium and Mary Jane Halsted of Canada. The *Revue* had already appeared at Madison Square Garden, Pittsburgh, and Chicago, before coming to St. Paul.[2]

Hibbing Junior Chamber of Commerce
Third Annual Ice Follies
TUESDAY, DECEMBER 28, 1937

PROGRAM

1—Markhus Ballet
2—Maxine Sheffer — Solo
3—Arthur Preusch, Jr. — Solo
4—Old Gray Mare Dorothy Franey and Miles Shilling
5—Margaret Grant — Solo
6—Melvin Doherty — Solo
7—Darline Peterson — Solo
8—Thomas Twins, Mary and Jane
9—Gordon Leary — Solo
10—Patricia Robb — Solo
11—Shirley Bowman and Angeline Knapp — Pair
12—Rosalind Smith — Solo
INTERMISSION
13—The Texas Ballet
14—Mary Louise Premer — Solo
15—Mr. and Mrs. Arthur Preusch — Pair
16—Jeannette Ahrens — Solo
17—Vic Etienne Comedy Solo
18—The Peasant Trio
Ardria Thomas, Mary Kay Harrington, Barbara Reynolds
19—Dorothy Franey Exhibition Speed Skating
(North American Champion)
20—Dr. J. N. Pike and Angeline Knapp — Pair
21—Shirley Bowman — Solo
22—Orrin Markhus and Irma Thomas
(Dancing Number)
23—Comedy Gordon Leary and Art Leary
24—Grand Waltz
25—Finale by Entire Company
Compliments of **HIBBING ADVERTISING CLUB**

Ice carnivals often presented programs mixing figure and speed skating, ice ballets, comic routines, and at least one pair of skaters dressed as a horse.

Above: Jack Horner designed the Winter Carnival Ice Court with its large rink for the Winter Carnival of 1938.

Right: Vivi-Anne Hultén co-starred with Karl Schaefer in a touring show, The Gay Blades Revue, featured during the Winter Carnival of 1938.

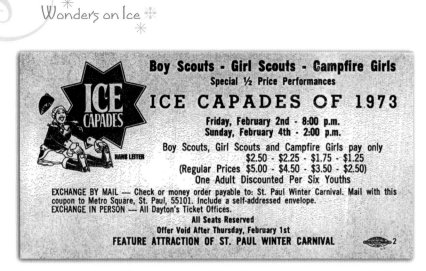

Boy Scouts - Girl Scouts - Campfire Girls
Special ½ Price Performances

ICE CAPADES OF 1973

Friday, February 2nd - 8:00 p.m.
Sunday, February 4th - 2:00 p.m.

Boy Scouts, Girl Scouts and Campfire Girls pay only
$2.50 - $2.25 - $1.75 - $1.25
(Regular Prices $5.00 - $4.50 - $3.50 - $2.50)
One Adult Discounted Per Six Youths

EXCHANGE BY MAIL — Check or money order payable to: St. Paul Winter Carnival. Mail with this
coupon to Metro Square, St. Paul, 55101. Include a self-addressed envelope.
EXCHANGE IN PERSON — All Dayton's Ticket Offices.

All Seats Reserved
Offer Void After Thursday, February 1st
FEATURE ATTRACTION OF ST. PAUL WINTER CARNIVAL

For many years the Ice Capades *came to St. Paul for appearances in the Auditorium during the Winter Carnival.*

Working with the St. Paul Figure Skating Club, the Winter Carnival hosted the U.S. National figure skating championships at the Auditorium in 1939. It was at this event that Robin Lee earned his fifth consecutive senior men's title. Following the Nationals, Lee joined the *Ice Capades* briefly and then entered military service. He returned to St. Paul after the war and became a figure skating coach at both the St. Paul FSC and the FSC of Minneapolis. That club's Midwest Open is now named for Robin Lee.

Since the St. Paul Figure Skating Club had ice time available in the summer, skaters from other towns and states came to St. Paul to practice or teach. Maribel Y. Vinson, nine-time American senior ladies' champion, came as a teacher and produced the first *Ice Cavalcade* for the Winter Carnival, in 1939. The show was pure skating—a mix of solos, pairs, and ice dancing routines. The *Ice Cavalcades* for 1941 and 1942 were directed by Canadian skater Montgomery "Bud" Wilson. Wilson was the nine-time Canadian men's champion and six-time North American senior men's title holder. His first year cast included the British world champion Megan Taylor, Edi Scholdan of Austria, and St. Paul's first champion Fours team. After a reduced effort in 1943, the Winter Carnival closed down until the war ended.

When the mayor of St. Paul, following the suggestion of a sportswriter, named a committee to honor athletes, the Winter Carnival Association was asked to arrange the event at the St. Paul Hotel. The honorees were those who had participated in national or international competitions. The Hamline University basketball team and four figure skaters made the list: John Lettengarver, Janette Ahrens, Madelon Olson, and Margaret Grant.[3]

In 1952, as a new event, the Winter Carnival featured a collaboration between the St. Paul FSC, the Saintpaulites Incorporated (producers of the Winter Carnival), and the Civic Opera Association, calling it *The "Call of the North" Revue*. Rudolph Friml's operetta, *Rose Marie*, was enacted on the stage of the Auditorium annex with singers and the Civic Opera orchestra, and on the ice by over one hundred skaters. Patsy Ann Buck and Margaret Grant alternated as the heroine. Dick Branvold and Martin Coonan took turns in skating the role of Jim Kenyon, her Mountie flame. Robin Lee was the skating director of *King Boreas XVI's Ice Revue*.[4]

While the *Ice Follies* always performed in Minneapolis at the Arena in the late spring (after hockey season ended), the *Ice Capades* (begun in 1941) arranged their tours to coincide with Carnival-time in St. Paul. Programs for both the *Ice Follies* and *Ice Capades* publicized their Minnesota skaters, both headliners and chorus members. Often tryouts were held in the Twin Cities for skaters who hoped to join either show.

In addition to the shows, there continued to be possibilities for the general public to skate during Carnival-time. In both 1956 and 1978 the block of 5th Street between Wabasha and St. Peter streets was flooded and frozen,

Schedule cover for the St. Paul Winter Carnival of 1980.

allowing anyone to skate there. The St. Paul FSC performed noon hour shows on Fifth Street ice. In 2005 and 2006 a temporary skating rink was erected on the Market Street side of Landmark Center.

Designs for Winter Carnival buttons occasionally showed skaters like the clown on the 1980 button. That year there was a convention of an international clown group during Carnival week. Other buttons have shown skaters in more traditional poses and costumes, like the Merry Ol' Tymes design of 1981 and the Norman Rockwell design on the 1982 button.

Parade floats have shown both skating and skates. Winter Carnival floats have transported skaters; a small skating rink was part of a Hamm's brewery float in 1970.

Parade Grand Marshals have represented the world of skating as well. Sarah Hughes, the Olympic gold medalist, took on that assignment in 2004. Snoopy had preceded her in the role in 1990. That year an exhibit of Charles Schulz's work was held in Landmark Center. Visitors to the exhibit were given flyers with two *Peanuts* strips reproduced. In one, Marcy and the famous beagle practiced pairs skating. In their unusual lift Marcy hoisted her partner aloft by his nose. The second strip

Wearing a Winter Carnival button indicated support for the festival, but also provided free entrance to many events.

Farwell Ozmun and Kirk's queen candidate rode in a giant skate on the company's 1939 float while other parade floats have carried small ice rinks for their passengers to use.

had Snoopy complaining that Woodstock, his small bird friend, would not let him drive the Zamboni on the ice. In the last panel Woodstock is shown at work. Naturally his ice rink was in a birdbath.

The Winter Carnival's most recent Ice Palace (built in 2004) faced the Xcel Energy Center where the All Star Hockey Game was held that year. Those who entered the palace's icy gates could skate on what was called the NHL Rink. Early on opening night of the Palace, visitors met the city's mayor, Randy Kelly, tracing graceful figures in the ice.

In January 2008, visitors to St. Paul will be able to enjoy both the annual Winter Carnival and the return of the U.S. Figure Skating Nationals to the city. The venue will be the Xcel Energy Center, less than a block away from where the Auditorium once provided a home for the 1939 championships.

Advance publicity for the U.S. Nationals began at the 2007 Minnesota State Fair. August 25th was designated as Figure Skating Saturday. Exhibitions, demonstrations by local figure skaters, and appearances by champions Nancy Kerrigan, Emily Hughes, and Eliot Halverson were part of the festivities in Carousel Park. The Winter Carnival royal family visited so that Boreas Rex LXXI (Don Schoeller) could knight Nancy Kerrigan. Minnesota skaters were asked to bring photographs to place on what will become a Minnesota Figure Skating Photo Wall for display at the Xcel Energy Center during the U.S. Nationals.[5]

✳ ❄ ✳ ❄ ✳ ❄ ✳ ❄

1. "Large Crowd Sees Best Rink Exhibit Ever Presented Here," *Rochester Post-Bulletin*, February 4, 1924.

2. *St. Paul Pioneer Press*, January 27, 1938, 12; and February 2, 1938, 1.

3. *St. Paul Pioneer Press*, April 1, 1945, 3: 1.

4. Program for the "Call of the North Revue," January 30-1, February 1, 1952. See also *St. Paul Pioneer Press* (January 27, 1952), Women's Section, 1.

5. "Skating Stars energize the fans," *St. Paul Pioneer Press*, August 26, 2007, 1, 3B.

Chapter Six

Competitions, Championships, and Acclaim

S katers must take the USFS tests if they want to compete at regional, sectional, and national competitions. The USFS determines which skills will be tested at each level and whether age limits should be established. USFS-affiliated skating clubs offer a testing program for the eight levels of proficiency with tests offered on a monthly schedule. Skaters who pass all eight levels are Gold Medalists; Silver Medalists have passed seven of the exams. While tests once focused on the famous figures, now these have been incorporated into what is known as "Moves in the Field." For someone watching the tests, the change has meant that a skater will complete the maneuvers over the entire length of the rink rather than being confined to a small patch area.

Skating judges who administer the tests follow rules published annually in the USFS Rulebook. Judges themselves undergo their own series of tests and written examinations, allowing them to evaluate skaters on beginning, advanced, and national levels. Eligible judges may then be selected by the USFS to serve on international panels as referees; some may also be asked to serve as team leaders. Coaches, who belong to the Professional Skaters Association headquartered in Rochester, Minnesota, have other tests to complete before they can receive that group's certification.

Each year skaters compete through regional and sectional championships. These are known as qualifying championships as the winners are qualified to move up to the next level of competition. For Minnesota skaters the competitions are known as the Upper Great Lakes Regional and Midwestern Sectional Championships or the "Uppers" and the "Mids." The next higher level contests are Nationals, Worlds, and, every four years, the Winter Olympics. From 1923-71 there were also the North American Championships held every other year for skaters from the United States and Canada. Since 1995 there has been a series of events, held in various cities throughout the world, known as the Grand Prix Championships. The junior

Harry Radix's Christmas cards often had a skating theme like this one celebrating the 1960 Olympic Games at Squaw Valley, California.

Grand Prix series of tournaments began in 1999. Skating federations assign teams whose members compete in two of the series of seven contests held in Europe, Asia, and the United States. Single skaters, pairs, and ice dancers with the highest marks based on their placements then compete in a series-ending event. Jennifer Karl, Ben Miller, and Eliot Halverson (St. Paul FSC) and Molly Oberstar (Duluth FSC) have represented theSUnitCd States in these junior Grand Prix events. Their assignments took them to Europe and Asia.

Several Minnesota clubs hold non-qualifying competitions annually. These include Skate St. Paul, the St. Cloud FSC's Granite City Classic, Northland (Duluth FSC), Hiawathaland (Rochester FSC), Braemar-City of Lake's Braemar-McCandless, Roseville's Roseville Classic, and the FSC of Minneapolis' Midwest Open, which is now the Robin Lee Midwest Open.

One award that has been given to U.S. national and international champions since 1937 is the Radix pin. Harry Radix, a former president of the Chicago FSC, longtime member of the USFSA board and a jewelry manufacturer, began the tradition. Radix died in 1965 but provided for the continued gift of Radix pins in his will.[1] Margaret Grant was one skater who received a Radix pin.

What follows is a list of competitions and championships that have been held in Minnesota with the dates, locations, and names of the individuals who have served as the chairs of the local organizing committees. *Skate America*, first held at Lake Placid in 1979, is the only international event held annually in the United States. Participants are senior level skaters.

A list of skaters who have become champions at the national level also follows. No Minnesota skaters have won either World or Olympic titles while affiliated with a Minnesota skating club. Jill Trenary, who first trained at the Lake Minnetonka FSC, won her titles after moving to Colorado. Others who have won national titles while members of figure skating clubs elsewhere include Robin Lee, who skated for either the Chicago FSC or the New York FSC when he won four of his five senior men's titles. Joanne Scotvold also skated with the Chicago club when she won her national novice ladies' title. Lyman Wakefield Jr. won both a national junior pairs title and a national junior dance championship (each with a different partner) as a member of the Skating Club of Boston.

Minnesota skaters earned gold medals in sectional, national, and North American championships in one discipline that no longer exists: the Fours. The idea was Canadian and it was through Montgomery Wilson that members of the St. Paul FSC originally learned about Fours. There were two teams. Janette Ahrens, Mary Louise Premer, Robert Uppgren, and Lyman Wakefield Jr. won their titles in 1940-41. Janet Gerhauser, John Nightingale, Marilyn Thomsen, and Marlyn Thomsen earned theirs from 1947-50. Fours competitions were never staged in World or Olympic championships.

Members of the two Fours teams competed as pairs, single skaters, and ice dancers, winning medals in each discipline. Janet Carpenter of the second Fours team remarked that club carnivals throughout the United States and Canada invited them to appear, as their four skaters could also skate as solos and in pairs.

A list of Minnesota State Champions (1980 through 2008) may be found in the Appendix.

Figure Skating Championships Held in Minnesota

U.S. National Championships

January 19-21, 1939. Sponsored by the USFSA. Hosted by the St. Paul FSC and the St. Paul Winter Carnival Association. Held at the St. Paul Auditorium. Arthur F. Preusch Sr., chair.

February 24-26, 1944. Sponsored by the USFSA. Hosted by the FSC of Minneapolis. Held at the Minneapolis Arena. Arthur F. Preusch Sr., chair.

March 26-29, 1958. Sponsored by the USFSA. Hosted by the FSC of Minneapolis. Held at the Minneapolis Arena. Lyman Wakefield Jr., chair.

January 22-27, 1973. Sponsored by the USFSA. Hosted by the FSC of Minneapolis, the St. Paul FSC and the Braemar FSC. Held at the Met Sports Center, Bloomington. Gil Holmes and John Klindworth, co-chairs.

February 13-17, 1991. Sponsored by the USFSA. Hosted by the TCFSA and Courage Center. Held at Target Center, Augsburg College Arena, and Parade Ice Garden, all in Minneapolis. Bruce Brayton and Anne Klein, co-chairs.

January 20-27, 2008. Sponsored by the USFSA. Hosted by the TCFSA. Held at Xcel Energy Center, St. Paul. Elizabeth Harty and Dann Krueger, co-chairs.

Uniform patch for the 1973 U.S. Nationals.

Tickets for the 1991 U.S. Nationals included the Opening Ceremonies, Competitions, and the Final Exhibition.

1991
UNITED STATES
FIGURE SKATING
CHAMPIONSHIPS

PRESENTED BY

Diet Sprite & NutraSweet

MINNEAPOLIS · ST. PAUL · MINNESOTA
FEBRUARY 10-17

Program and logo for the U.S. Nationals of 1991.

**St. Paul Civic Center
October 14–20, 1985**

SKATE AMERICA 1985

ST. PAUL/MINNEAPOLIS

...bell's® Soups

PRESENTS:

SKATE AMERICA INTERNATIONAL '85

INSIDE:
- Salute to the 50th anniversary of the St. Paul Figure Skating Club
- Spectators Guide to Figure Skating
- You Be The Judge—The Perfect "6"
- Plus photos of Skate America competitors

Sticker and program for Skate America '85.

Other Significant Championships Held in Minnesota

Skate America '85

October 14-20, 1985. Sponsored by the USFSA and the ISU. Hosted by the TCFSA. Held at the St. Paul Civic Center. Bette Snuggerud, chair.

Snowflake International Invitational Precision Competition

January 2-3, 1993. Sponsored by the USFSA. Hosted by the TCFSA. Held at the Met Sports Center, Bloomington. Marlys Larson and Etta Jane Belrose, co-chairs.

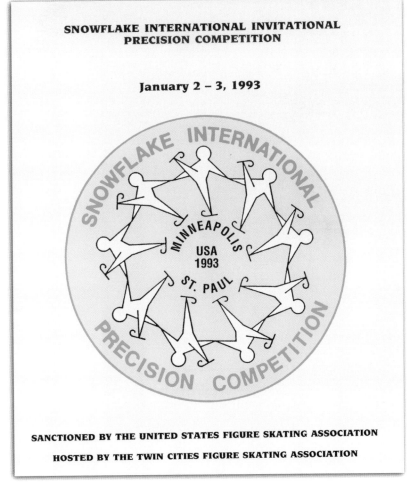

Highstepping, handholding figures emphasize the nature of this precision (now synchronized) skating event on its program cover.

*The patch and program for the 1998 World Figure Skating
Championships used a logo that symbolized the patterns a skater traces
on ice against the blue of a city by the water.*

World Figure Skating Championships

March 29-April 5, 1998. Sponsored by the ISU and the USFSA. Hosted by the TCFSA. Held at Target Center and Parade Ice Garden, both in Minneapolis. Jimmy Disbrow, chair.

World Synchronized Skating Championships

April 5-8, 2000. Sponsored by the ISU and USFSA. Hosted by the TCFSA. Held at Mariucci Arena, University of Minnesota, and Parade Ice Garden, both in Minneapolis. Marlys Larson, chair.

This handbook for the World Synchronized Skating Championships gave skaters, coaches, and judges all the necessary information.

Minnesota's National Champions

Senior Men, Combined:

1926 - Chris I. Christenson, Twin City FSC

1939 - Robin H. Lee, St. Paul FSC

Senior Men, Figures:

1993, 1994 - Gig Siruno, St. Paul FSC

Fours:

1940 - Mary Louise Premer, Robert Uppgren, Janette Ahrens, Lyman Wakefield Jr., St. Paul FSC

1947 - Janet Gerhauser, John Nightingale, Marilyn Thomsen, Marlyn Thomsen, St. Paul FSC

1948 - Janet Gerhauser, John Nightingale, Marilyn Thomsen, Marlyn Thomsen, St. Paul FSC

1950 - Janet Gerhauser, John Nightingale, Marilyn Thomsen, Marlyn Thomsen, St. Paul FSC

Junior Men:

1932 - Robin H. Lee, Twin City FSC

1933 - William Swallender, FSC of Minneapolis

1935 - Earl Reiter, Twin City FSC

1942 - Walter Sahlin, FSC of Minneapolis

1946 - John Lettengarver, St. Paul FSC

2007 - Eliot Halverson, St. Paul FSC

Junior Ladies, Free Skate:

1994 - Jennifer Karl, St. Paul FSC

Junior Ladies, Combined:

1931 - Margaret Bennett, FSC of Minneapolis

1944 - Madelon Olson, St. Paul FSC

1990 - Alice Sue Claeys, Braemar-City of Lakes FSC

Junior Pairs:

1943 - Betty Schalow and Arthur F. Preusch Jr., St. Paul FSC

1947 - Harriet Sutton and John Lettengarver, St. Paul FSC

1950 - Janet Gerhauser and John Nightingale, St. Paul FSC

Novice Men, Free Skate:

2006 - Eliot Halverson, St. Paul FSC

Above: Janet Gerhauser and John Nightingale won the national junior pairs title and went on to compete at the Oslo Olympic games in 1952, placing sixth.

Left: In a snowbank are several St. Paul FSC national champions holding their trophies: Janette Ahrens, Robert Uppgren, Arthur Preusch Jr., and Betty Schalow.

Novice Men, Combined:
> 1941 - Walter Sahlin, FSC of Minneapolis
> 1945 - John Lettengarver, St. Paul FSC
> 1947 - Marlyn Thomsen, St. Paul FSC

Novice Ladies, Free Skate:
> 2006 - Rhiana Brammeier, St. Paul FSC

Novice Ladies, Combined:
> 1952 - Mary Ann Dorsey, St. Paul FSC
> 1976 - Kelsy Ufford, FSC of Minneapolis

Novice Dance:
> 1991- Nicole Dumonceaux and John Reppucci, Braemar-City of Lakes FSC

The Bedell Harned Trophy was awarded to the St. Paul Figure Skating Club in 1947 since that club had earned the most points for medals won by its skaters of any club in national competition that year. The Trophy recognized the national Fours championship won by Marlyn and Marilyn Thomsen, John Nightingale and Janet Gerhauser; the national junior pairs crown won by Harriet Sutton and John Lettengarver; Marlyn Thomsen's national novice crown; and the silver medals earned by Janette Ahrens in the national senior ladies' championship and John Lettengarver in the national senior men's championship.

National Collegiate Champions

Senior Ladies, Free Skate:
> 1992 - Sara Kastner, University of St. Thomas
> 1993 - Sara Kastner, University of St. Thomas
> 1997 - Kimberly Cole, University of Minnesota

Junior Ladies, Free Skate:
> 1993 - Wendy Budzynski, Augsburg College
> 2004 - Rachel Baisch, Macalester College

U.S. Open Professional Champions

The U.S. Open Championships began in 1980 and were last held in 1997.

> 1986 - Tracy Shulman
> 1988 - Kathleen Schmelz
> 1992 - Jill Trenary
> 1994 - Gregor Filipowski

The St. Paul FSC members who earned the Harned Trophy from left to right are Marlyn Thomsen, Marilyn Thomsen, John Lettengarver, Janette Ahrens, Harriet Sutton, John Nightingale, and Janet Gerhauser.

North American Champions

The North American Championships were held every other year from 1923 to 1971.

Fours:

1941 - Janette Ahrens, Robert Uppgren, Mary Louise Premer, Lyman Wakefield Jr., St. Paul FSC

1949 - Janet Gerhauser, John Nightingale, Marilyn Thomsen, Marlyn Thomsen, St. Paul FSC

International Competitions for Junior and Novice Skaters

Grand Prize SNP

Banská Bystrica, Czechoslovakia

Junior Ladies:

1983 - Jana Sjodin, St. Paul FSC

Pokal der Blauen Schwerter (Blue Swords)
Chemnitz, Germany

Junior Ladies:
1989 - Robyn Petroskey, St. Paul FSC

Gardenia Spring Trophy
Ortisei, Italy

Junior Ladies:
1994 - Jennifer Karl, St. Paul FSC

North American Challenge Skate
Location alternates between the United States and Canada

Junior Ladies:
2001 - Kristen Sheaffer, St. Paul FSC
2002 - Jillian Asby, Eden Prairie, FSC
2005 - Kirsten Olson, FSC of Bloomington

Novice Men:
1997 - Rohene Ward, St. Paul FSC
1998 - Matt Wesenberg, FSC of Bloomington
1999 - Benjamin Miller, St. Paul FSC

Triglav Trophy
Jesenice, Slovenia

Novice Men:
2005 - Eliot Halverson, St. Paul FSC

Young International
Luxembourg

Novice Ladies:
2005 - Christina Maria Sperduto, Braemar-City of Lakes FSC

Midwestern Champions

The Midwestern Section includes eighteen states, reaching from Alabama and Texas to Minnesota, North Dakota, Wisconsin, and Michigan. A Minnesota skater qualifies for the sectional tournament by medaling in the regional tournament, the Upper Great Lakes. Midwestern Championships have been held in Bloomington (1996, 1999), Edina (1990), Minneapolis (1935, 1955, 1960, 1972, 1981, 1984), and Rochester (1948). The Midwestern Championships began in St. Louis in 1933.

Senior Men:
- 1933 - Robin Lee, Twin City FSC
- 1935 - Earl Reiter, Twin City FSC
- 1942, 1943, 1944 - Arthur Preusch Jr., St. Paul FSC
- 1946, 1947 - John Lettengarver, St. Paul FSC
- 1949, 1950 - Marlyn Thomsen, St. Paul FSC
- 1999 - Danny Clausen, St. Paul FSC

Senior Ladies:
- 1933 - Ann Haroldson, Duluth FSC
- 1939 - Shirley Bowman, St. Paul FSC
- 1943, 1944, 1945, 1946 - Janette Ahrens, St. Paul FSC
- 1947 - Joanne Scotvold, FSC of Minneapolis
- 1953, 1954 - Mary Ann Dorsey, St. Paul FSC
- 1961 - Vicky Fisher, FSC of Minneapolis
- 1978 - Kelsy Ufford, FSC of Minneapolis
- 1986 - Jana Sjodin, St. Paul FSC
- 1995 - Robyn Petroskey, St. Paul FSC
- 2000 - Katie Lee, St. Paul FSC

Senior Pairs:
- 1933 - Edith and Arthur Preusch Sr., Twin City FSC
- 1942, 1943 - Janette Ahrens and Robert Uppgren, St. Paul FSC
- 1944 - Janette Ahrens and Arthur Preusch Jr., St. Paul FSC
- 1946, 1947 - Harriet Sutton and John Lettengarver, St. Paul FSC
- 1949, 1950, 1951 - Janet Gerhauser and John Nightingale, St. Paul FSC
- 1952 - Patsy Ann Buck and Martin Coonan, St. Paul FSC
- 1964 - Barbara Hartwig and Bobby Mecay, St. Paul FSC
- 1996, 1997 - Cheryl Marker and Todd Price, St. Paul FSC

Senior Dance:

    1933 - Edith and Arthur Preusch Sr., Twin City FSC

    1939, 1941 - Edith and Arthur Preusch Sr., St. Paul FSC

Senior Precision or Synchronized Teams:

    1989 - Minneapple Corps, FSC of Minneapolis

Fours:

    1950 - Janet Gerhauser, John Nightingale, Marilyn Thomsen, Marlyn Thomsen, St. Paul FSC

Junior Men:

    1939 - Robert Uppgren, St. Paul FSC

    1941 - Bruce Scheffer, St. Paul FSC

    1942 - James Lawrence, St. Paul FSC

    1945 - John Lettengarver, St. Paul FSC

    1960 - Bobby Mecay, St. Paul FSC

    1990 - Gig Siruno, St. Paul FSC

    2001 - Rohene Ward, St. Paul FSC

    2007 - Eliot Halverson, St. Paul FSC

Junior Ladies:

    1942 - Margaret Grant, St. Paul FSC

    1952 - Mary Ann Dorsey, St. Paul FSC

    1975, 1976 - Kathy Gelecinskj, FSC of Minneapolis

    1980 - Beth Ann Carolin, Rochester FSC

    1983 - Jana Sjodin, St. Paul FSC

    1989 - Robyn Petroskey, St. Paul FSC

    1990 - Alice Sue Claeys, Braemar-City of Lakes FSC

    1994 - Jennifer Karl, St. Paul FSC

    1997 - Sarah Call, FSC of Bloomington

    2003 - Kristin Sheaffer, St. Paul FSC

Junior Pairs:

    1943 - Betty Schalow and Arthur F. Preusch Jr., St. Paul FSC

    1951 - Patsy Ann Buck and Martin Coonan, St. Paul FSC

    1963 - Judy James and Lowell Green, FSC of Minneapolis

    1974 - Rose Mary Wilzbacher and Rick Turley, St. Paul FSC

    1994 - Cheryl Marker and Todd Price, St. Paul FSC

Junior Precision or Synchronized Teams:

2006 - Team Braemar, Braemar-City of Lakes FSC

2007 - Team Braemar, Braemar-City of Lakes FSC

Novice Men:

1948 - Arnold Savage, St. Paul FSC

1976 - Stuart Bailey, FSC of Minneapolis

1999 - Benjamin Miller, St. Paul FSC

2006 - Eliot Halverson, St. Paul FSC

Novice Men, Figures:

1991 - Anand Bokde, St. Paul FSC

Novice Ladies:

1945 - Joyce Scotvold, FSC of Minneapolis

1971 - Betsy Hobson, Braemar-City of Lakes FSC

1974 - Kathy Gelecinskj, FSC of Minneapolis

1976 - Kelsy Ufford, FSC of Minneapolis

1982 - Jana Sjodin, St. Paul FSC

1988 - Robyn Petroskey, St. Paul FSC

2001 - Kristen Sheaffer, St. Paul FSC

2006 - Rhiana Brammeier, St. Paul FSC

Novice Ladies, Figures:

1994 - Katie Grinnell, St. Paul FSC

1996 - Bethany Peterson, St. Paul FSC

Novice Pairs:

1971 - Rose Mary Wilzbacher and David Bolton, St. Paul FSC

Novice Dance:

1991 - Kimberly Callahan and Robert Peal, Braemar-City of Lakes

Intermediate Men:

1985 - Grant Rorvick, St. Paul FSC

1995 - Jeremy Allen, St. Paul FSC

Intermediate Ladies:

1972 - Kathy Gelecinskj, FSC of Minneapolis

International Competitions for Synchronized Teams

MILK International Precision
Helsinki, Finland

Senior:
1990 - Minneapplettes, FSC of Minneapolis

Novice:
1990 - Mini-Minneapplettes, FSC of Minneapolis

Snowflake Trophy
Zagreb, Croatia

Junior:
2007 - Team Braemar, Braemar-City of Lakes FSC

The Centennial Luncheon

When Minnesota celebrated its Statehood Centennial in 1958, one scheduled event focused on athletes. Sports writers and other interested parties selected a list of 1,958 individuals who had made their mark on the sporting calendar as athletes, coaches, or writers. The banquet program, held on May 5, 1958, listed those chosen by county, town, and sport. Among the skaters were Eddie and Roy Shipstad, Heinie Brock, Arthur F. Preusch Sr., Lyman Wakefield Jr., Robin Lee, John Nightingale, John Strauss, Raymond F. Kelly, and Earl Reiter.

The 1980 Winter Olympics

Mention the 1980 Winder Olympic Games held at Lake Placid and talk inevitably turns to the unforgettable, classic championship hockey game played between the United States and Russia. Filled with Minnesota players and coached by Herb Brooks of the University of Minnesota, the underdog U.S. team triumphed, and their victory became known as The Miracle on Ice.[2] But other Minnesotans had taken center stage at Lake Placid even before the Games began. A precision skating team, assembled from various Minneapolis clubs, took part in the opening ceremonies. Precision skating, now called "synchro," was not widely known at the time and the Minnesota team was proud to have presented its skills to a worldwide audience.

World and Olympic Teams

Skaters who have won or medaled in a National Championship may be selected for the World or Olympic teams. Those who have been chosen for the Olympic squad include Robin Lee whose trip would have been in 1940, but was cancelled, John Lettengarver, John Nightingale, Janet Gerhauser, Jill Trenary, and Earl Reiter. For the World teams, the selection committees chose Lee, Lettengarver, Janette Ahrens, Nightingale, Mary Ann Dorsey, Vicky Fisher, Jill Trenary, and Janet Gerhauser.

Team leaders, already mentioned, accompany skaters to the championships. Tamie Campbell, who has had that assignment, said she became both a cheerleader and a travel agent, being supportive of her skaters and making sure arrangements ran smoothly. Team leaders know the system, have friends throughout the skating community, and thus help their skaters understand the business of competitive skating. Ms. Campbell has judged in Paris, Japan, the Czech Republic, Slovakia, Romania, and Sweden. Judges are usually invited to serve on two international panels per year in the fields they evaluate (hers are singles and pairs).

Judges often benefit from experience as competition skaters. Janet Gerhauser Carpenter was a member of the 1952 Olympic team as a pair skater with John Nightingale. She then served as an Olympic team leader at Sarajevo in 1984 and as an Olympic judge at Calgary in 1988 (for the Battle of the Brians) and at Salt Lake City in 2002.

A happy team of precision skaters awaits their bus ride to the Winter Olympic games at Lake Placid in 1980.

The USFSA Hall of Fame

The governing council of the USFSA voted in 1975 to establish a Figure Skating Hall of Fame with selections to be completed by the following year. Three categories of nominees were chosen: amateur skaters who had been outstanding competitors or had made noteworthy contributions in style or technique; individuals who had served the sport in a non-skating capacity (such as judges, coaches, administrators); and those whose importance came from their involvement as professional skaters.[3] A Hall of Fame medal showing each of figure skating's four disciplines was given to each new member of the Hall of Fame. Eddie Shipstad and Oscar Johnson were in the first group of inductees.[4] Minnesota members of the Hall of Fame are:

1976 - Eddie Shipstad, Oscar Johnson
1995 - Robin H. Lee, Roy Shipstad
1998 - Evy Scotvold, Tom Collins
2002 - Jill Trenary
2005 - Mary Louise Premer Wright
2007 - Charles M. Schulz
2008 - Janet Gerhauser Carpenter

ISI Ice Skating Hall of Fame

1964 - Kenneth Bartholomew
1965 - Eddie Shipstad Sr., Roy Shipstad, Oscar Johnson
1969 - Morris Chalfen
1971 - "Old Smoothies," Irma Thomas and Orrin Markhus
1972 - Everett McGowan
1979 - Paul Riedell

The ISI National Merit Award was given to Barb Yackel in 2001.

PSA Awards

The professional coaches organization has created several awards which have been given to judges, referees, coaches and others in the skating community. Minnesota honorees are:

Distinguished Judges/Referees:
1999 - Janet Gerhauser Allen
2000 - Mary Louise Premer Wright

Lifetime Achievement and Honorary Members:

    1970 - Roy Shipstad, Eddie Shipstad, Oscar Johnson

    1973 - Wally Sahlin

    1974 - Snoopy

    1984 - Paul Riedell

    1989 - Carole Shulman, David Shulman

Coaches Hall of Fame:

    2001 - William Swallender

❄ ❄ ❄ ❄ ❄ ❄ ❄ ❄

1. Benjamin T. Wright. *Skating in America: The 75th Anniversary of the United States Figure Skating Association* (1996), 64.
2. A bronze statue of Herb Brooks was placed outside the Rice Park entrance to River Center after the coach's death. Brooks is shown raising both arms high as he did when he realized his team had won.
3. Benjamin T. Wright. *ibid*, 266.
4. Wright, *ibid*, 276.

Chapter Seven

The Learning Curve: Teachers, Coaches, and Judges

Teachers

Classes and individual instruction have been offered by almost every club. Several independent schools where skating was taught have also operated in the metropolitan area. The first was a studio owned by Dorothy Lewis (1921-2002) at 2929 Emerson Avenue South, near the Minneapolis Arena. Lewis, born in St. Paul, had skated with the St. Paul FSC and in local shows, before turning professional as a teenager. She joined the *Ice Capades* and was featured in the *Ice Capades of 1941* movie. From 1938 through the 1940s, she starred in ice shows in the Iridium Room of the St. Regis Hotel in New York City and in the Copley Plaza Hotel in Boston.[1] During the summers she returned to Minnesota where she directed and starred in a similar tank (or small ice rink) show at the Hotel Nicollet. A program for her *Adventures on Ice* (1941) show, held on the Minnesota Terrace of the Nicollet Hotel, credits choreography to Harry Lossee and music direction to Jack Pfeiffer. Both were associated with Sonja Henie for many years, with her films as well as her shows.

Miss Lewis offered classes for children, working girls, and married women plus coaching for those who hoped to have a career in professional skating such as she had. Her studio was small, but there was a rink, and space to learn choreography with a ballet barre, mirrors, and a music box. Carole Shulman, former director of the Professional Skaters Association, called Lewis a "consummate show woman" who choreographed other events and sometimes lent costumes to skaters who needed them. While some Twin Cities skaters took part in Ms. Lewis' shows, most of her cast members were veterans of similar hotel tank shows.

Above: Autographed publicity photograph for the Ice Capades (1941). Dorothy Lewis skated with the Ice Follies, toured with the Ice Capades and starred in their film. Later, using a portable rink she toured with a small cast of skaters on the West Coast.

Opposite page, top to bottom: A flyer for her skating school (circa 1951), a program for one of her shows on the Minnesota Terrace of the Hotel Nicollet (1943), and a table tent advertisement for another edition of her productions (1944).

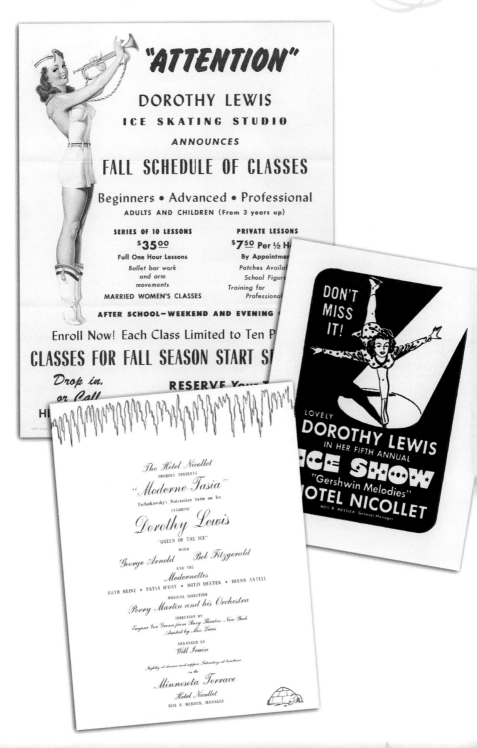

Dorothy Lewis' Home Skating Rink went on sale in the 1950s.

Dorothy Lewis had her own traveling rink, a gift from her husband. She also marketed a portable outdoor skating rink, intended for installation in backyards. A booklet that accompanied the rink kit gave ideas on creating colored ice with vegetable dyes, games to play on the ice, and the first ten lessons in Lewis' "how to skate" program.

Many articles and photographs about Dorothy Lewis appeared in newspapers and magazines. She also endorsed products as other athletes and actors of the time did. One product she favored was Camel cigarettes. In one undated advertisement, she is shown skating (a camel spin) and is also shown seated in her skating costume of a white silk dress and a silver fox turban. She holds a pack of Camels and is quoted as saying, "If my nerves were jittery, I couldn't keep my performance up to par. Whirlwind spins and turns put constant pressure upon my nerves. So whenever I can, I break nerve tension, I let up—and light up a Camel."

Vivi-Anne Hultén (1911-2003) came to Minnesota for the first time in 1938 to star in an ice skating show for the St. Paul Winter Carnival (see Chapter Five). As a show skater she headlined appearances of the *Ice Vanities* company in the northern Minnesota towns of Hibbing and Duluth in 1940. She returned to St. Paul to coach skaters for the Pop Concerts in the summer of 1941. The ten-time Swedish national champion and Olympic bronze medalist (1936) skated with the *Ice Capades* and *Holiday on Ice* after marrying Gene Theslof. In *Holiday on Ice* shows, she and her husband skated as an adagio pair doing a number much like the "Old Smoothies" routine of Orrin Markhus and Irma Thomas but with lifts added at the end. While the Theslofs were touring with *Holiday on Ice*, the show's Opening Night in Indianapolis in 1963 became a disaster.[2] A gas explosion

A special camera captured the speed of Vivi-Anne Hultén's spin while she practiced for an ice show at Madison Square Garden in 1940.

Vivi-Anne Hulten's

FUN & PLEASURE
SKATING SCHOOL

Presents

"FUN on ICE"

ALDRICH ARENA'S
Fifth Annual Spring Ice Revue

on

April 22 and 23, 1967

at

7:30 p.m.

THE PRODUCTION IS SANCTIONED
BY THE UNITED STATES FIGURE
SKATING ASSOCIATION THROUGH
THE COURTESY OF THE ST. PAUL
FIGURE SKATING CLUB, MEMBERS
OF WHICH ARE FEATURED IN THE
SHOW.

Hundreds of children attended Vivi-Anne Hultén's skating school and took part in the revues that she directed and choreographed beginning in 1967.

occurred. Seventy-four spectators were killed and four hundred were injured. When they received an invitation to come to St. Paul, they accepted and left the show. Vivi-Anne Hultén had been asked by Ed Furni of the St. Paul Auditorium to work again with the St. Paul Pop Concerts. This would lead eventually to other coaching and teaching positions for her.

In 1967 Vivi-Anne Hultén founded her Fun and Pleasure Skating School at Aldrich Arena. As one reporter described it:

Right: Bona Dai Beckstrom and Vivi-Anne Hultén practice for a St. Paul Pop Concert in 1966.

Below: Barb Yackel and Rose Mary Wilzbacher were the Little Girl Pair in the "Gone West" number of Fun on Ice of 1967.

Last year she opened the doors at Aldrich and the response was terrific. 60 tiny tots, 500 other youthful and adult skaters three times a week at the arena, hoping some day, maybe, one of the youngsters will follow in her footsteps and reach Olympic heights.[3]

She taught skating for over thirty years, until she was in her eighties. If a child could walk, she felt, that tot could learn to skate. For those who were still a bit wobbly on their feet she invented a pusher they could grab for balance. She had tiny skates made with Strauss blades attached for those in her Babes on Ice classes. Hundreds of children learned to skate in her program and at least a few would go on to play high school and college hockey such as the Brodt sisters, Chelsey and Winny.

Close scrutiny enabled a judge to evaluate a skater's "figures," as Jane Fleming is doing at the Midwesterns of 1971.

Holding the judges' marks in the old scoring system used at the Midwesterns of 1971.

Stories about Vivi-Anne Hultén always mentioned her rivalry with Sonja Henie and her suspicions that the Norwegian skater did not always win fairly.[4] Ms. Hultén's own record was significant with her ten Swedish national titles and three bronze or silver world titles, her career in the traveling ice shows, and her success as a teacher. Many Minnesotans remember the ageless white-haired skater effortlessly soloing to the strains of Debussy's "Clair de Lune." And they remember the stress she placed on posture, on silent strokes, on "patting the ice," as her friend Genny Burdette recalled, and the lessons she taught based on her background in ballet. Some of her students assisted her and later became teachers and coaches like Jerre Sweno LeTourneau and Barb Yackel.

The third school was also the creation of a former professional skater. Michael Kirby, a Canadian, had won the junior men's championship of his country before turning professional. He skated with the *Ice Follies*, then with Sonja Henie's company as leading man, and with Barbara Ann Scott in the London production of *Rose Marie*. He decided to open a skating school on the order of the Fred Astaire and Arthur Murray dance schools. His first skating school, called the Ice Chalet, opened in Chicago. Like the dance academies, it was a franchise operation and the Minnesota example was briefly located at the Ice Center in Minneapolis. Those who wanted to teach went to Chicago to learn Kirby's system. Kirby became the first president of the Ice Skating Institute of America (ISIA), whose headquarters are in Dallas, Texas.

Judges

Every club that offers a testing program keeps a list of eligible test judges. This is the responsibility of the club officer known as the test chair. "Judges," wrote Christine Brennan, "are the most misunderstood people in figure skating."[5] Unknown to the general public, often criticized, and, of course, very powerful since their decisions can so thoroughly affect a skater's career, judges do their work as volunteers, and are paid only for their expenses. Judges often choose to contribute their time for many years. Judges accredited to evaluate international competition must retire at age seventy, but no upper age limit exists for local, test, and national judges. They are usually skaters, sometimes with experience as national and international competitors, as Janet Carpenter had.[6] They learn by serving an apprenticeship as trial judges, seeing whether the marks they would give equal those given by their mentors. There are yearly exams to pass and judges' schools to attend. Annual USFS Rulebooks explain what skills each year's skaters will have to demonstrate

Janet Gerhauser and John Nightingale often practiced at Williams Arena. Here they sit with their coach Robin Lee between them.

in tests and competitions. The 2006 USFS Directory listed forty-one Minnesotans who can judge either tests or competitive events. Mary Louise Premer Wright and Lyman Wakefield Jr., of the first St. Paul Fours, and Jane Lincoln are among those who marked fifty years as judges. C.I. Christenson of the Twin City FSC had the most unusual experience in judging in 1926 when he competed and won the senior national men's title and judged three other events.[7]

Minnesotans who have judged Olympic and world competitions include Lyman Wakefield Jr., Mary Louise Premer Wright, Janet Gerhauser Carpenter, Jane Fleming Lincoln, and Tamie Klindworth Campbell.

Other opportunities to assist in the operations of figure skating come to those who have entered the world of judging. Each competition has referees and often team leaders who escort skaters to the events. Although these positions are not salaried, still the opportunity to accompany a team to an Olympic competition or to be on the team of judges assigned to international or national meets is an extraordinary opportunity. As judges say, it is a way to give back to the sport that they feel has benefited them.

Josephine Lawless, who skated with both the St. Paul FSC and the University of Minnesota FSC (she was president of that club in 1955-56), became a judge after college. Ms. Lawless had skated in the St. Paul Pop

Concerts but had no interest in joining one of the ice shows. Friends in California, where she moved and still lives, urged her to become a judge. In 1974 she was the first woman to serve as Chief Referee at a U.S. Nationals. Another first was to head the USFSA committee on competitions (1984-86). She continues to judge singles and pairs at the national level. Thinking of her early years in skating, she said, "It was a unique time for St. Paul skaters. We stayed in the sport even if we moved away because it has been a good experience. We were supportive of each other."

Coaches

Every club has one or more coaches on staff. Minnesota skaters have been fortunate over the years to study with coaches like Robin Lee, Vivi-Anne Hultén, Barbara Kossowska, Felix Kaspar, Maribel Vinson, Pierre Brunet and Andrée Joly, to name a few famous names. Other coaches have trained and competed with local clubs, then turned to coaching, like Jean Pastor, Ted Engelking, Jerre LeTourneau, Janet Hoitomt, Kathleen Schmelz, Joan Orvis, and Carole Shulman.

Coaches, like judges, have often competed as singles, pairs, or ice dancers. The Professional Skaters Association (PSA), headquartered in Rochester, Minnesota, since 1985, is their organization. It offers training

Coach Ann Eidson works with skaters as young as Val Hart at the St. Paul FSC.

Increasing competition opportunities now exist for elite skaters. Coach Ted Engelking poses with skater Eliot Halverson at the Junior Grand Prix in Budapest, (2006), where Eliot placed third.

and accreditation for those who want to coach through the clubs or independently. Course work with oral and written exams can lead to several levels of certificates: registered, certified, senior, and master's. The work can be taken in various disciplines: choreography, dance, pairs, moves in the field, free skating, and synchronized skating. All course work involves some focus on sports medicine.

First known as the American Skaters Guild, the PSA was founded in 1938. Changes in leadership often meant changes in the location of its offices with moves made from Colorado Springs, Colorado, to Lake Placid, New York, to Buffalo, New York. Carole Shulman, who had just retired from coaching with the Rochester FSC, was asked to become the executive director of the PSA and so the headquarters moved to Rochester. Both Carole and her husband David had long been coaches; David served as president of the PSA from 1974-77 and later as its legal counsel.

On June 8, 2001, the PSA opened its new headquarters building in the Allegro Park Plaza Complex. In front of the handsome glass building and on display inside its Headquarters Gallery are bronze sculptures of skaters done by Douglas and Meghan Taylor-Gebler. As part of the dedication, a skating exhibition by Kristi Yamaguchi, Renée Roca, Gorsha Sur, and others took place at the Rochester-Olmsted County Recreation Center. The current executive director of the PSA is Jimmy Santee.

Lacing his skates is Dick Vraa who coached for the Rochester FSC in the 1960s and later for the FSC of Minneapolis.

At the threshold of the season of FIRE,

Come rejoice in the wonder of ICE.

CELEBRATION

Invitation

Invitation designed by Joseph Davidson for the dedication of the Professional Skaters Association headquarters in Rochester, 2001.

Figures and Patches

In *The Mikado* Nanki-Poo introduces himself as a wandering minstrel with the words, "A thing of shreds and patches, of ballads, songs, and snatches, and dreamy lullaby!" Music is, of course, an integral part of skating, both competitive and theatrical, and so once was the patch, although not in the sense Nanki-Poo means.

A patch was a rectangle measuring 20 by 45 feet. The ice rink was divided into patches, each one of which could be purchased for an hour of practice. In 1956 the St. Paul FSC printed its schedule. Each day there were five hour-long patch sessions available at a cost of seventy-five cents each. A skater signed up for patches in order to practice figures. At each testing level a skater had to master a certain number of figures and then, in competition, be able to demonstrate whichever figures (out of the list of dozens) had been chosen. Skaters had to be able to skate a figure and then retrace precisely that same figure in the same lines three times. Judges, and coaches, spent a great deal of time looking carefully at the edges and turns traced.

For the skater it was usually a quiet work time. Each person concentrated on doing the figures in his or her patch, but there were rinks where the experience was not quite that. At the St. Paul Arena, the orchestra for the Pop Concerts might be there practicing as well, so Dorothy Curtis remembers it as

> … a bewitching atmosphere. We filled our patches with
> school figures while a clarinet tooted richly forth or a
> French horn sang a passage from a composition soon
> to be played. We free skated quietly in the great space
> and soft light, hearing each other's blades—a toe pick
> chopping a divot through the new thin ice, the rasp of a
> scratch spin, a sibilant cross-foot, the zip of a take-off
> and the thud of a landing—or, when the orchestra
> played, we whirled around, exhilarated out of our
> minds, improvising moves to the music (and dodging
> each other) until forced to stop for breath.[8]

While Maribel Vinson was in St. Paul to produce the *Ice Cavalcade* show for the St. Paul Winter Carnival she wrote an article for a local magazine about the upcoming 1939 U.S. Nationals. She hoped that readers would choose to watch the school figures, especially the senior men's or women's sessions because of the high caliber of skating they would see. She advised her readers:

> As you watch them, notice how they skate the figures,
> whether their posture is erect, easy, and graceful,
> whether they place the lines of their second and third
> circles close on top of the original diagram (each figure
> must be skated three times over on each foot), and
> whether the size of the figure as a whole is small and
> puny, large and sprawling, or seemingly well suited to
> the physique of the skater. For on all of these points the
> judges will be basing their marks.[9]

She felt that several Minnesota skaters would do well, but she was sure that "tall, handsome, blond" Robin Lee would win the senior men's title again, as he did. Of Lee, she wrote, "Today he is, in my opinion, the greatest male skater the United States has yet produced."[10]

The world divided up into patches ended when the USFS decided to change the rules. Skaters had always learned the figures and demonstrated their mastery of them in competition. Some skaters were

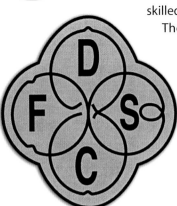

The patch once worn by members of the Duluth FSC incorporates several of the famous school figures.

skilled at figures, others were far better at free skating. The superior figure skater almost always won, however, since the higher score (60 percent of the final amount) was awarded to the skater of figures. This was puzzling to audiences, especially when television began showing championships. Skaters doing their figures were never shown because television producers considered it boring. Yet when the crowd witnessed an exciting free skating performance and then learned that the skater who had just done that did not win because of a low score in the unseen figure competition, the reaction forced the national organization to take another look at the way competitions were being judged.

Gradually, over a twenty-year span, the power of the figures waned. Once figures no longer counted or were even expected to be learned, coaches no longer focused their students' time on learning them. Setting aside patch time for practice became unnecessary. Eventually the patch no longer meant a division of space on an ice rink, but rather cloth membership logos to be sewn to a jacket.

There were dissenting voices. Vivi-Anne Hultén felt that figures were the basis of the sport. She wrote:

> School figures are supposed to teach skaters techniques: to handle those steel blades, balance on them, hold a steady edge and use all four edges; how to master various leans, quick changes of direction, intricate turns (rockers, brackets, counters, loops), and footwork of all kinds. All this is supposed to be a background for freeskating; how to get the proper edge and consequent pressure for the take off of jumps; how to land after jumps, go into and out of spins, etc.[11]

Others preferred the intricate tracing of delicate edges to jumps which seemed to reek of gymnastics and not skating. But the change had happened. Judges and coaches had to learn what was included in the new "Moves in the Field." Judges also had to learn a new system in scoring with scores so rapidly recorded by computer that a skater's presence in the "kiss and cry" seats is shorter than ever. The last competitive compulsory figures were skated at the World Championships in Halifax,

Nova Scotia, in 1990 when Jill Trenary won the senior ladies' title. James Hines wrote, "No single entity had greater influence on their discontinuance than television."[12]

* * * * * * * *

1. "Supper Club Darling," *St. Paul Pioneer Press*, The Show Magazine, March 16, 1941, 12.
2. John H. Harvey. "She's Kept Her Career on Ice for Decades," *St. Paul Pioneer Press*, April 14, 1974, Lively Arts Magazine, 4.
3. Jim Walsh. "Lost Her Medal, but Got Her Man," *St. Paul Dispatch*, November 5, 1968, 3.
4. See John H. Harvey. "She's Kept Her Career on Ice for Decades," *ibid*; Katherine Lanpher. "Original Skating Feud a Vivid Memory," *St. Paul Pioneer Press*, February 17, 1994, 1; and Ozzie St. George, "66-Year-Old Skater Warms to Life on the Ice," *St. Paul Pioneer Press*, November 13, 1977, 8-9.
5. Christine Brennan. *Inside Edge* (1996), 70.
6. Jay Welner. "High court presides over skaters," Minneapolis *Star Tribune*, February 11, 2002, C10.
7. Benjamin Wright. *op. cit.*, 3
8. Dorothy Snell Curtis. *Changing Edges*, 12.
9. Maribel Vinson. "Can You Spot the Champion?" *Golfer and Sportsman*, January 1939, 26.
10. Vinson, *ibid*, 61.
11. Vivi-Anne Hultén. "What Happened to Figure Skating's School Figures?" *Skating*, October 1984, 35.
12. James Hines. *op. cit.*, 235.

Appendix
Minnesota State Champions

Since 1980 TCFSA has staged a non-qualifying competition for Minnesota skaters affiliated with local clubs. Minnesota skaters who are members only of the USFS are termed Individual Members and may also compete. This listing contains the first place winners. Gaps in the listing may indicate a lack of information, but more often suggest that no competition in that discipline at that level was held.

Senior Men:
 2002 - Rohene Ward, Starlight Ice Dance Club

Senior Ladies, Free Skating:
 1991 - Alice Sue Claeys, Braemar-City of Lakes FSC
 1993 - Angela Rothmund, St. Paul FSC
 1994 - Kristin Knotts, St. Paul FSC
 1995 - Wendy Budzinski, St. Paul FSC
 1996 - Kimberly Cole, St. Paul FSC
 1997 - Sara Kastner, St. Paul FSC
 1998 - Kimberly Cole, St. Paul FSC
 1999 - Jennifer Karl, St. Paul FSC
 2000 - Katie Lee, St. Paul FSC
 2001 - Heidi Pakkala, FSC of Bloomington
 2002 - Angie Lien, Duluth FSC
 2003 - Angie Lien, Duluth FSC
 2004 - Angie Lien, Duluth FSC
 2005 - Angie Lien, Duluth FSC
 2006 - Angie Lien, Duluth FSC
 2007 - Kendra Keenan, Braemar-City of Lakes FSC
 2008 - Molly Oberstar, Duluth FSC

Senior Ladies, Combined:
1982 - Ann Olson, St. Paul FSC
1983 - Kathleen Schmelz, FSC of Minneapolis
1984 - Kris Morzinski, FSC of Minneapolis
1986 - Jill Anderson, FSC of Minneapolis
1989 - Michele Forner, Lake Minnetonka FSC
1990 - Sara Kastner, St. Paul FSC

Senior Ladies, Figures:
1991 - Crissy Giles, Rochester FSC
1994 - Gretchen Stump, St. Paul FSC

Junior Men:
1996 - Steve Kirby, Burnsville-MN Valley FSC
1998 - Rohene Ward, St. Paul FSC
1999 - Matt Wesenberg, FSC of Bloomington
2000 - Rohene Ward, FSC of Minneapolis
2002 - Viktors Bariss-Ayele, Starlight Ice Dance Club
2003 - Viktors Bariss-Ayele, Starlight Ice Dance Club

Junior Ladies, Free Skating:
1991 - Bridgit Ryan, St. Paul FSC
1992 - Bridgit Ryan, St. Paul FSC
1993 - Lisa Bell, St. Paul FSC
1994 - Jamie Lea Lund, Rochester FSC
1995 - Annika Gill, Rochester FSC
1996 - Heather Johnson, St. Paul FSC
1997 - Sarah Call, FSC of Bloomington
1998 - Kristy Harris, St. Paul FSC
1999 - Heidi Pakkala, FSC of Bloomington
2000 - Tanya Traut, Alexandria FSC
2001 - Steffie Smith, Eden Prairie FSC
2002 - Kristen Sheaffer, Starlight Ice Dance Club
2003 - Jillian Asby, Eden Prairie FSC
2004 - Stephanie Zastrow, St. Paul FSC
2005 - Molly Oberstar, Duluth FSC
2006 - Kristina Olson, St. Paul FSC
2007 - Kirsten Olson, FSC of Bloomington
2008 - Kirsten Olson, Individual Member

Junior Ladies, Combined:
> 1980 -Tina Sjodin, FSC of Minneapolis
> 1981 - Lynette Larson, Braemar-City of Lakes FSC
> 1982 - Judy Hoel, FSC of Minneapolis
> 1983 - Jana Sjodin, St. Paul FSC
> 1984 - Theresa Pilarski, FSC of Minneapolis
> 1985 - Paula Ruppell, St. Paul FSC
> 1986 - Kathryn Curielli, FSC of Minneapolis
> 1987 - Beth Sonderup, FSC of Minneapolis
> 1988 - Tei Lea Kano, FSC of Minneapolis
> 1990 - Alice Sue Claeys, Braemar-City of Lakes

Junior Ladies, Figures:
> 1992 - Genia Hesser, Rochester FSC
> 1994 - Kelly Wald, St. Paul FSC

Novice Men:
> 1994 - Steve Kirby, Apple Valley FSC
> 1996 - Kelly Smith
> 1997 - Jeremy Allen, Braemar-City of Lakes FSC
> 1998 - Benjamin Miller, St. Paul FSC
> 2002 - Ryan Yearous, Braemar-City of Lakes FSC
> 2004 - Paul Wood, Rochester FSC
> 2005 - Paul Wood, Rochester FSC
> 2008 - T.J. Yang, St. Paul FSC

Novice Ladies, Free Skating:
> 1991 - Annika Gill, Rochester FSC
> 1992 - Carrie Halgrimson, St. Paul FSC
> 1993 - Annika Gill, Rochester FSC
> 1994 - Heather Johnson, St. Paul FSC
> 1995 - Courtney Sayther, FSC of Bloomington
> 1996 - Angie Lien, Duluth FSC
> 1997 - Katie Nuszloch, Rochester FSC
> 1998 - Anne Michaletz, Braemar-City of Lakes FSC
> 1999 - Tanya Traut, Alexandria FSC
> 2000 - Courtney Green, Eden Prairie FSC
> 2001 - Kristen Sheaffer, St. Paul FSC
> 2002 - Anna Buller, Braemar-City of Lakes FSC
> 2003 - Stephanie Zastrow, St. Paul FSC

2004 - Molly Oberstar, Duluth FSC
2005 - Kirsten Olson, FSC of Bloomington
2006 - Christina Maria Sperduto, Braemar-City of Lakes FSC
2007 - Kate Charbonneau, FSC of Bloomington
2008 - Kiri Baga, FSC of Bloomington

Novice Ladies, Combined:

1980 - Jana Sjodin, FSC of Minneapolis
1981 - Janee Cusick, Maplewood FSC
1982 - Jill Trenary, Lake Minnetonka FSC
1983 - Denise Wind, FSC of Minneapolis
1984 - Dawn Victorson, FSC of Bloomington
1985 - Tracey Scherer, Braemar-City of Lakes FSC
1986 - Susie Saari, FSC of Minneapolis
1987 - Robyn Petroskey, St. Paul FSC
1988 - Stephanie Hillstrom, FSC of Minneapolis
1989 - Kelly Sullivan, FSC of Minneapolis
1990 - Gretchen Stump, St. Paul FSC

Novice Ladies, Figures:

1991 - Gretchen Stump, St. Paul FSC
1992 - Kelly Grant, Rochester FSC
1993 - Leah Kerrigan, Rochester FSC
1994 - Molly Cornelison, St. Paul FSC
1995 - Heather George, St. Paul FSC
1996 - Bethany Peterson, St. Paul FSC
1997 - Jenny Borman

Intermediate Men, Free Skating:

1989 - Bill Annear, St. Paul FSC
1998 - Ryan Yearous, St. Paul FSC
1999 - Eric Sandstrom, St. Paul FSC
2000 - Aaron Garside, St. Paul FSC
2001 - Aaron Garside, St. Paul FSC
2002 - Paul Wood, Rochester FSC
2003 - Paul Wood, Rochester FSC
2005 - Alex Johnson, Braemar-City of Lakes FSC
2006 - Garrett Kling, Chaska FSC
2008 - Alex Zadeii, St. Paul FSC

Intermediate Men, Combined:

 1985 - Brian Schmidt, Rochester FSC

Intermediate Men, Figures:

 1995 - Matt Wesenberg, FSC of Bloomington

Intermediate Ladies, Free Skating:

 1986 - Jenni Sauer, FSC of Minneapolis
 1989 - Annika Gill, Rochester FSC
 1991 - Kellie Dean, St. Paul FSC
 1992 - Heather Johnson, St. Paul FSC
 1993 - Lisa Krygier, Rochester FSC
 1994 - Angie Lien, Duluth FSC
 1995 - Heidi Pakkala, FSC of Bloomington
 1996 - Katrina Kehoe, Duluth FSC
 1997 - Steffie Smith, St. Paul FSC
 1998 - Tanya Traut, Alexandria FSC
 1999 - Kristen Sheaffer, St. Paul FSC
 2000 - Jillian Asby, Eden Prairie FSC
 2001 - Stephanie Zastrow, St. Paul FSC
 2002 - Stephanie Zastrow, St. Paul FSC
 2003 - Katie Pennington, The Heights FSC
 2004 - Kirsten Olson, FSC of Bloomington
 2005 - Amanda Farris, FSC of Bloomington
 2006 - Kate Charbonneau, FSC of Bloomington
 2007 - Kiri Baga, FSC of Bloomington
 2008 - Shannon Brakke, Rochester FSC

Intermediate Ladies, Combined:

 1980 - Debbie Hill, St. Cloud FSC
 1981 - Tammy Dumstorff, Rochester FSC
 1982 - Bernadette Watowich, Duluth FSC
 1983 - Lisa Cornelius, FSC of Minneapolis
 1984 - Maria Fragomeni, Roseville FSC
 1985 - Britt Larson, Burnsville-MN Valley FSC
 1986 - Tei Lea Kano, FSC of Minneapolis
 1987 - Nanette DeBrule, St. Paul FSC
 1988 - Amy Nornig, FSC of Minneapolis
 1989 - Kelly Grant, Rochester FSC
 1990 - Carrie Halgrimson, St. Paul FSC

1991 - Jamie Lea Lund, Rochester FSC
1992 - Lisa Krygier, Rochester FSC
1993 - Lisa Krygier, Rochester FSC
1994 - Molly Bullis, Burnsville FSC

Intermediate Ladies, Figures:

1991 - Shannon Simonson, Eden Prairie FSC
1992 - Sarah Frost, Duluth FSC
1993 - Katie Grinnell, St. Paul FSC
1994 - Molly Bullis, Burnsville FSC
1995 - Kimberly McLachlan

Intermediate Dance Pairs:

1983 - Jill Harstad and John Hilger
1988 - Kim Hartley and Ross Lyons

Juvenile Men/Open Juvenile Men:

1993 - Kyle Gill, Rochester FSC
1994 - Matt Wesenberg, Bloomington FSC
1996 - Rohene Ward, Starlight Ice Dance Club
1999 - Pablo Vielguth, Roseville FSC
2003 - Eliot Halverson, St. Paul FSC
2004 - Garrett Kling, Chaska FSC
2006 - Alex Zadeii, St. Paul FSC
2008 - Ryan Santee, Rochester FSC

Juvenile Men, Figures:

1984 - Kevin Hilger, Maplewood FSC
1989 - Bill Annear, St. Paul FSC
1993 - Kyle Gill, Rochester FSC

Juvenile Girls:

1980 - Jana Sjodin, St. Paul FSC
1983 - Maria Fragomeni, Roseville FSC
1984 - Robyn Petroskey, St. Paul FSC
1991 - Kari Barbo, St. Paul FSC
1992 - Emily Ziemer
1993 - Sarah Call, FSC of Bloomington
1994 - Heidi Pakkala, FSC of Bloomington
1995 - Airina Rodrigues, St. Paul FSC

1996 - Steffi Smith, St. Paul FSC
1997 - Alyssa Kane, Braemar-City of Lakes FSC
1998 - Kristina Olson, Braemar-City of Lakes FSC
1999 - Jillian Asby, Eden Prairie FSC
2000 - Stephanie Zastrow, St. Paul FSC
2001 - Kendra Keenan, Braemar-City of Lakes FSC
2002 - Alison Hoyer, Rochester FSC
2003 - Kirsten Olson, FSC of Bloomington
2004 - Arianne Thomas, St. Paul FSC
2005 - Delanie Honda, Braemar-City of Lakes FSC
2006 - Jacy Meyer, St. Paul FSC
       Kiri Baga, Duluth FSC
2007 - KayCee Nelson, St. Paul FSC
       Alana Christie, FSC of Bloomington
2008 - Jillian Christie, FSC of Bloomington

Juvenile Girls, Combined:

1980 - Jana Sjodin, St. Paul FSC
1981 - Lesley Ann Beha, St. Paul FSC
1982 - Kathryn Curielli, FSC of Minneapolis
1983 - Maria Fragomeni, Roseville FSC
1984 - Robyn Petroskey, St. Paul FSC
1985 - Danielle Olthoff, FSC of Minneapolis
1986 - Lisa Levine, Braemar-City of Lakes FSC
1987 - Jennifer Dvorak
1988 - Annika Gill, Rochester FSC
1989 - Debbie Thompson
1990 - Delia Johnson
1991 - Sarah Frost, Duluth FSC
1992 - Kate Cook, St. Paul FSC
1993 - Lindsy Halleckson, St. Paul FSC
1994 - Bethany Peterson, St. Paul FSC

Juvenile Girls, Figures:

1991 - Sarah Frost, Duluth FSC
1992 - Beth Swanson
1993 - Lindsy Halleckson, St. Paul FSC
1994 - Bethany Peterson, St. Paul FSC
1995 - Elizabeth Brown, Duluth FSC

Juvenile Dance:
2005 - Mackenzie Ross and Logan Mohs, Vacationland FSC

Open Juvenile Ladies:
1991 - Rachel Hinman
1992 - Gara Gambucci, Braemar-City of Lakes FSC
1993 - Molly Bullis, Burnsville-MN Valley FSC
1994 - Candice Pearson
1995 - Jeannine Nelson, FSC of Minneapolis
1996 - Cassie Glover, FSC of Minneapolis
1997 - Kelly McCool, Braemar-City of Lakes FSC
1998 - Anne Lindberg, Roseville FSC
1999 - Kristin Erb, Eden Prairie FSC
2000 - Brittany Proctor, Roseville FSC
2001 - Erin Kilbury, Eden Prairie FSC
2002 - Dana Goldamer, Eden Prairie FSC
2003 - Kinsey Kleppe, Eden Prairie, FSC
2004 - Rachel Ann Nelson, Rochester FSC
2005 - Kristina Hermansen, Lake Minnetonka FSC
2006 - Katlyn Tarras, Eden Prairie FSC
2007 - Maddie Haggerty, St. Paul FSC
2008 - Tesslina Trejo, Rochester FSC

Open Juvenile Ladies, Figures:
1986 - Kjerstin Moody
1987 - Tanya Kroeplin
1994 - Leah Micheletti, Bloomington FSC

Open Pre-Juvenile Men/ Pre-Juvenile Men:
1992 - Ryan McKone
1993 - Ryan Will, Burnsville-MN Valley FSC
1997 - Andrew Wong, Rochester FSC
2001 - Michael Chau, St. Paul FSC
2002 - Alex Johnson, Braemar-City of Lakes FSC
2004 - Carl Johnson, Rochester FSC
2007 - Daniel Kulenkamp, St. Paul FSC

Open Pre-Juvenile Men/ Pre-Juvenile Men, Combined:
1988 - Bobby Kaping, Burnsville-MN Valley FSC

1989 - Steve Kirby, Burnsville-MN Valley FSC
1990 - Keith Gramsted
1992 - Ryan McKone
1993 - Ryan Will, Burnsville-MN Valley FSC

Open Pre-Juvenile Men/ Pre-Juvenile Men, Figures:

1992 - Chris Peterson
1993 - Adam Collins, Bloomington FSC

Open Pre-Juvenile Ladies:

1991 - Callie Lipkin, Lake Minnetonka FSC
1992 - Kisha Richburg, Maplewood FSC
1993 - Rhys Conlon, Bloomington FSC
1994 - Kiaja Morgenthaler, Bloomington FSC
1995 - Katherine Hatch, Burnsville-MN Valley FSC
1996 - Sarah Levitt, St. Paul FSC
1997 - Sarah Wall, Rochester FSC
1998 - Emily McGlynn, Braemar-City of Lakes FSC
1999 - Shannon Gilbertson, Lake Minnetonka FSC
2000 - Serena Horsager, Burnsville-MN Valley FSC
2001 - Kayla Kamrath, St. Paul FSC
2002 - Nichole Bjornstad, The Heights FSC
2003 - Angie Bromeland, St. Paul FSC
2004 - Melanie Sarkissian, Maplewood FSC
2005 - Rose Roberts, Maplewood FSC
2006 - Maddie Haggerty, St. Paul FSC
2007 - Jill DeFiel, St. Paul FSC

Open Pre-Juvenile Ladies, Figures :

1994 - Kiaja Morgenthaler, Bloomington FSC
1995 - Brooke Ahlquist

Pre-Juvenile Ladies:

1991 - Emily Ziemer
1992 - Jessica Haugsland
1993 - Kelly Lynn Hanly, Rochester FSC
1994 - Christina Pautz, Braemar-City of Lakes FSC
1995 - Courtney Swalboski, Duluth FSC
1996 - Tara Gilmer, St. Paul FSC
1997 - Julia Dunn, Braemar-City of Lakes FSC

1998 - Catherine Cakir, Braemar-City of Lakes FSC
1999 - Dana Peterson, Burnsville-MN Valley FSC
2000 - Lauren Elyse Anderson, Braemar-City of Lakes FSC
2001 - Sabrina Logren, Roseville FSC
2002 - Katelyn Meyers, Roseville FSC
2003 - Delanie Honda, Braemar-City of Lakes FSC
2004 - Meghan Stonefield, Eden Prairie FSC
2005 - Jacy Meyer, St. Paul FSC
2006 - KayCee Nelson, St. Paul FSC
2007 - Madison Rothweiler, FSC of Bloomington
2008 - Hannah Peterson, St. Paul FSC

Preliminary Boys:

2000 - A. J. Moghaddam, FSC of Bloomington
2001 - Eliot Halverson, St. Paul FSC
2002 - Alexander Marchenko, The Heights FSC
2003 - Garrett Kling, Chaska FSC
2004 - Samuel Moghaddam, Braemar-City of Lakes FSC
2005 - Ryan Brammeier, St. Paul FSC
2006 - Cale Ambroz, New Prague FSC
2007 - Colton Johnson, FSC of Bloomington
2008 - Jackson Kelner, Braemar-City of Lakes FSC

Preliminary Girls:

1986 - Jennifer Wald, FSC of Minneapolis
1995 - Miia Rasinen, FSC of Minneapolis
1996 - Jessica Horner, Rochester FSC
1997 - Kelly Dutcher, Braemar-City of Lakes FSC
1998 - Ann Marie Nielsen, Eden Prairie FSC
1999 - Kelly Sullivan, Braemar-City of Lakes FSC
2000 - Rebecca Hughes, Braemar-City of Lakes FSC
2001 - Rhiana Brammeier, St. Paul FSC
2002 - Christina Maria Sperduto, Braemar-City of Lakes FSC
2003 - Jessica Fisher, Maplewood FSC
2004 - Amanda Luchau, St. Paul FSC
2005 - Maria Kalina, Starlight Ice Dance Club
2006 - Kate Geschwind, Rochester FSC
2007 - Jillian Christie, FSC of Bloomington
2008 - Bailey Sernett, FSC of Bloomington

Preliminary Dance Pairs:

    1981 - Lesley Ann Beha and Cory Cardenas, St. Paul FSC

Preliminary Pairs:

    1981 - Gina Burdette and Geoffrey Patrick, Maplewood FSC

    1984 - Molly Hilger and Kevin Hilger

Precision or Syncro Senior Teams:

    1983 - Braemarettes, Braemar-City of Lakes FSC

    1984 - Minneapplettes, FSC of Minneapolis

    1986 - Minneapplettes, FSC of Minneapolis

Precision or Syncro Junior Teams :

    1983 - Braemarettes, Braemar-City of Lakes FSC

    1986 - Shamrocks, FSC of Bemidji

    1988 - Minneapplettes, FSC of Minneapolis

Precision or Syncro Novice Teams:

    1983 - Minnetonka Precision Line, Lake Minnetonka FSC

    1984 - Minnetonka Precision Line, Lake Minnetonka FSC

    1985 - The Pixies, St. Paul FSC

    1986 - Scotties, Braemar-City of Lakes FSC

    1987 - Mini-Minneapplettes, FSC of Minneapolis

    1988 - Mini-Minneapplettes, FSC of Minneapolis

Precision or Syncro Juvenile Teams:

    1986 - Mini-Mates, Lake Minnetonka FSC

Logo used for the 2007 TCFSA Minnesota State Championships in 2006.

Bibliography

Brennan, Christine. *Champions on Ice: Twenty-Five Years of the World's Finest Figure Skaters*. Plattsburgh, NY: McClelland & Stewart Ltd (2002).

Brennan, Christine. *Inside Edge: A Revealing Journey into the Secret World of Figure Skating.* New York: Scribners (1996).

Brokaw, Irving. *The Art of Skating*. New York: Charles Scribner's Sons (1926).

Champions on Ice: 2006 Tour Program. Minneapolis: Tom Collins Enterprises.

Curry, Marion R. "Memories of a Golden Moment," Manuscript (2007).

Curtis, Dorothy Snell. "Changing Edges," *In Their Words: Stories of Minnesota's Greatest Generation*. Minnesota Historical Society. Temporarily online at www.mngreatestgeneration.org.

Gerhauser Carpenter, Janet. "A Woman on Ice: My Life in Figure Skating," in *Stories by Minnesota Women in Sports: Leveling the Playing Field*, edited by Kathleen C. Ridder, Jean Brookins, and Barbara Stuhler. St. Cloud, MN: North Star Press of St. Cloud (2005), 9-22.

Hines, James R. *Figure Skating: A History*. Urbana and Chicago: University of Illinois Press and Colorado Springs, CO: USFSA and the World Museum of Figure Skating (2006).

Johnson, J. Herbert. "Growing Up in Chisago City: One Man's Recollection of Boyhood Memories," Manuscript (2005).

Kelly, Raymond F., Papers. Minnesota Historical Society.

Kirby, Michael. *Figure Skating to Fancy Skating: Memoirs of the Life of Sonja Henie*. Raleigh, NC: Pentland Press Inc. (2000).

Kempner, Diane. "When Skating was Hipp," *Minnesota Monthly*, December 1986, 67-78.

Lambert, Luna. *The American Skating Mania: Ice Skating in the Nineteenth Century*. Exhibition catalogue, National Museum of History and Technology, December 1978-February 1979. Washington, DC: Smithsonian Institution (1978).

Larson, Paul Clifford. *Icy Pleasures: Minnesota Celebrates Winter*. Afton, MN: Afton Historical Society Press (1998).

Lindahl, Laurel. "Ice Cycles: The evolution of figure skating," *New Sweden Minnesota Program,* edited by Marcia Appel, (1988), 33-36.

Ogilvie, Robert S. *Competitive Figure Skating: A Parent's Guide.* New York: Harper and Row, Publishers (1985).

Olson, Sigurd F. *The Singing Wilderness*. New York: Alfred A. Knopf (1976).

Ridder, Kathleen C. "Escaping the Heat on a Summer Night. The St. Paul Figure Skating Club and Those Popular Summer Pop Concerts," *Ramsey County History* 34: 2 (Summer 1999), 4-12.

Shipstads and Johnson *Ice Follies* Collection. Minnesota Historical Society.

Shulman, Carole. *The Complete Book of Figure Skating.* Champaign, IL: Human Kinetics (2002).

Smith, Russell Scott. "Loop Dreams," *Minnesota Monthly* 32:3 (March 1998), 85-88, 137-139.

Strait, Raymond, and Leif Henie. *Queen of Ice, Queen of Shadow: The Unsuspected Life of Sonja Henie.* New York: Stein and Day (1985).

Strauss Skates Inc. Company Records. Minnesota Historical Society.

Turnquist, William E. "History and Development of the Rochester Figure Skating Club." Manuscript, n.d.

Uppgren, Robert. Papers. Minnesota Historical Society.

U.S. Figure Skating Association. *The Official Book of Figure Skating.* New York: Simon & Schuster Editions (1998).

Whedon, Julia. *The Fine Art of Skating*. New York: Harry N. Abrams Inc. (1988).

Wright, Benjamin T. *Skating in America: 1921-1996. The 75th Anniversary History of the United States Figure Skating Association*. Colorado Springs, CO: United States Figure Skating Association (1996).

Index